PEOPLE LIKE YOU

Stories for the Heart

L. Michael Schoonover

Copyright © 2024 By L. Michael Schoonover

All Rights Reserved

PEOPLE LIKE YOU

The book, *People Like You*, is a collection of inspirational stories about real life experiences of everyday people. These stories will draw the reader into a comfortable, non-threatening climate of pleasurable reading that when introduced, the reader will be self encouraged to continue reading.

I believe that *People Like You* will become a book that readers will be drawn to read, recommend, and read again. Readers will repeatedly recognize people much like themselves or someone familiar or family.

The book's prime purpose is to encourage all readers alike to initiate or rekindle relationships with the Almighty God. The intended message of *People Like You*, that God is real and alive, is delivered in a non-confrontational format that each reader can identify and not be offended. Without a doubt, I believe that *People Like You* will become a book read for its positive influence on the lives of many Americans, one life at a time.

It is noted here that all Bible Scriptures quoted or referred to in the writing of *People Like You* are from the Authorized Version or the King James Version of the Holy Bible. Names of present-day people have been altered to protect their identities. The author has utilized various means of punctuation and writing patterns to emphasize identification of highlighted details.

CONTENTS

PEOPLE LIKE YOU 3

A TIME FOR ALL SEASONS 8

THOUGHTS OF A PASSING SHEPHERD 14

#1. COME WHAT MAY, I WILL LOVE HIM 'TIL MY DYING DAY 17

#2. WHEN GOD REALLY SPOKE TO A MAN 19

#3. W HAT MANNER OF MAN IS HE? (Mk. 4: 41) 24

#4. WOMEN IN THE SHADOW OF CHRIST 27

#5. WHERE ARE YOU IN THE CHRISTIANS' OUTREACH OF THE CHURCH? 30

#6. IS GOD'S STILL SMALL VOICE LOUD ENOUGH FOR YOU TO HEAR? 32

#7. COURAGE TO STAND, FOR THAT WHICH IS RIGHT 34

#8. O, SAY CAN YOU SEE? 37

#9. HOW WELL DO YOU KNOW THIS STORY? 39

#10. CAN PEOPLE SEE YOUR FATHER IN YOU? 42

#11. HOW GREAT IS YOUR FAITH? 44

#12. ARE YOU ONE OF THE HARVEST OR ONE OF THE LABORERS? 48

#13. THE LONGER WE WAIT, THE GREATER THE COST 51

#14. ARE YOU GOING, TELLING, BAPTIZING, OR JUST FISHING? ... 53

#15. MAY YOUR DREAMS COME TRUE 56

#16. WHAT IS THE FOCUS OF OUR FAITH? 58

#17. A LIFE AS AN OPEN BOOK 62

#18. ATTRIBUTES OF A LOVING SAVIOR 65

#19. A LESSON OF HUMILITY 68

#20. HOW SKILLED ARE YOU WITH YOUR SWORD? 71

#21. HOW WAS YOUR HARVEST THIS YEAR? 74

#22. DIRECTIONS FOR USING ONE'S SWORD 77

#23. DO YOU UNDERSTAND THE PARABLES? 84

#24. THE DANGER OF NOT PRODUCING FRUIT 85

#25. WHAT WOULD THE FINGER OF GOD WRITE ABOUT US? 87

#26. PREPARE FOR A MIRACLE TODAY 92

#27. MAKE READY FOR A CHANGE IN LIFE 96

#28. HAVE YOU YOUR WEDDING INVITATION? 99

#29. ARE YOU LOOKING FOR A DIVERSION? 101

#30. LOVE WORTH SHARING 103

#31. WHEN ALL ELSE FAILS, READ THE DIRECTIONS 105

#32. MAKING THE MOST OF YOUR LIFE 108

#33. ARE YOU READY FOR THE SOUND OF A TRUMPET? 110

#34. WHEN WE CHECK HIM HERE AND CHECK HIM THERE 113

#35. I WISH I COULD HAVE BEEN THERE 115

#36. A PROMISE GIVEN IN GOD'S NAME IS A PROMISE 118

#37. WHICH GATE DO YOU WISH TO ENTER? 121

#38. SEEK WHILE THE LORD MAY BE FOUND 124

#39. ASK THE RIGHT PERSON AND YE SHALL RECEIVE 128

#40. WHAT IS YOUR CONCEPT OF ETERNITY? 130

#41. WHAT KIND OF FRIEND, ARE YOU? 132

#42. KEEP ME IN YOUR WILL SO I WON'T BE IN YOUR WAY 135

#43. PREPARE TO MEET THY GOD 138

#44. HOW ARE OUR LIVES REFLECTING THE SEASONS
OF LIFE? 141

#45. THE DESIRE FOR GREATNESS 143

#46. FELLOWSHIP WITH GOD IN THE GARDEN 146

#47. AN AFTERNOON WITH GOD ALONG FOR THE RIDE 150

#48. AN OPEN MIND ON AN OPEN HIGHWAY 152

#49. LET'S TAKE OUR STAND WITH SWORD IN HAND 156

#50. DEATH AS A GATEWAY TO PASS THROUGH 160

#51. HOW STORM WORTHY IS YOUR LIFE? 163

#52. SPOKEN TO BY THE GREAT I AM	166
#53. ARE YOU LISTENING FOR THE TRUMPET?	170
#54. THE PASSION OF CHRIST PASSED TO OTHERS	172
#55. DO YOU WISH YOU COULD HAVE BEEN THERE?	175
#56. UTILIZE TIME WHILE THERE IS TIME	180
#57. THE LIABILITIES OF A WEAKENING WITNESS	183
#58. DO YOU KNOW ANY GOOD NEWS TO SHARE?	189
#59. IT'S "SAFE" TO NOT ALWAYS SPEAK "OUT"	192
#60. PREPARING FOR BATTLE AGAINST THE ENEMY	195
ABOUT THE AUTHOR	201

A TIME FOR ALL SEASONS

Some years back before I was called to the ministry, I sensed that someday God might call me to preach. Since I had taught adult Bible class for several years and especially enjoyed the studying and sharing, I longed for the anticipated time that God might call me into His ministry.

When that time actually came to pass, His calling FRIGHTENED me TERRIBLY. I found myself in the presence of a Being that I KNEW that I was UNQUALIFIED to stand in His presence. I therefore refused to accept the call for fear of failure for some five years. When He again called me to preach, He toned Himself down dramatically to reduce my fear.

At the time God chose to restate His intentions to me about preaching, my wife and I had our eldest daughter married and our younger daughter in college at West Virginia University. Because when our elder daughter was in college, Sue and I had purchased her an automobile for her senior year. Leigh, our younger daughter, was now excited about the same for her.

Leigh, now entering her senior year, had already begun searching for her right car. I promised her that when she located a possible car, then I would go with her to see if it were a suitable vehicle to purchase. She took me into Pennsylvania, Morgantown, Boone

County, Charleston, and a few other places that I have forgotten. This process of searching for the right automobile consumed about six weeks. Several people in our county knew that Sue and I were looking for a vehicle for Leigh and at times, we received calls about some possible automobiles for Leigh and me to check out on the weekends when she sometimes came home.

On a Wednesday, someone at the bank called Sue to tell her that they had just received a title on an especially attractive Grand Am that would surely impress Leigh. After looking at the Grand Am, Sue and I knew that this would be the one for Leigh. Unfortunately, the bank would not hold the car until the weekend so Leigh could see it firsthand. Also, I had promised Leigh that I would not purchase an automobile for her without her seeing it first. Knowing that this automobile would be gone in a day or two, we decided to make the purchase. On the way home, we stopped at NAPA and purchased various cleaning, waxing, polishing supplies to hopefully enhance the automobile's appearance for Leigh when she came home on Friday.

Before starting to work on the automobile, I called Leigh. I repeated my promise and apologized for not letting her see the vehicle before purchase. I spoke, tearfully, "Leigh, you just have to trust me on this one." Leigh, so typical in her response, acknowledged her approval and said that she looked forward to Friday.

I returned outside to work enthusiastically on cleaning the inside and outside to maximum quality. As I was scrubbing the inside carpet with foam cleaner, God began to speak through my thoughts, about the ministry. I was so preoccupied with the condition of the automobile for Leigh that I tried to put the thoughts of a ministry out of my mind. Then I realized that my thoughts of the ministry were not my thoughts, but God's. I became overwhelmed and once again started to cry. Just as clearly as if He were standing there beside me, God spoke into my thoughts, "You just have to trust me on this one, Son." These were the very words that I had spoken to Leigh. Weeping uncontrollably, I stepped out of the back seat where I was cleaning and spoke to Sue, my wife, "I have to preach the Gospel. Do you want to go with me?"

I had run and avoided discussions with anyone, God included, for the past five years. Here, without any discussion or warning, I gave Sue fifteen seconds to make up her mind if she were going with me. How foolish and selfish of me? However, she answered positively, and we embarked on the greatest adventure of my life.

Later in the evening, I retired to an isolated area and prayed. I would sometimes talk aloud as well as through my prayers to Him. I constantly expressed my INABILITIES to be qualified to preach.

Through my thoughts, HE AGREED WITH ME. Yet, He calmed me and patiently prepared me for the ministry. I studied to show myself approved. As in preparing to teach, I believed that I needed more time than normal to understand fully a message to share with the church and begged Him not to allow me to enter the pulpit only to change the message. This was my greatest fear of being in the pulpit with a message that I had not sufficiently prepared for preaching.

One day I received a call to preach a revival that included seven back-to-back sermons. I went straight to God in prayer and

ARROGANTLY told Him that He knew that I needed more time between sermons, and why did He allow this call to be made. His answer was to trust Him. I found myself in waters that I had NEVER been in before.

I prepared for two weeks to preach the first message of the revival. The first night went well. God saved two people. I came back home and spent the remaining part of the night studying to preach the second night. I went to my daytime job and returned home to quickly review the message before going to the services.

That night I was a failure in my mind NOT SENSING HIS PRESENCE. However, another person came forward to be saved. Later, I was told by another preacher in the congregation that as I preached for 40 minutes, he had prayed for me the entire time.

When I returned home, I went to my study and leveled my frustration to a most tolerant and patient God. I lashed out as a frustrated child. When I finished and quieted myself, I prayed again, this time more calmly. I asked what I had done wrong. He calmly pointed out my failures to which I knew were correct. That night I learned to walk and preach by faith the ministry I had thought was mine. Before I retired for the evening, I realized that this ministry was not mine, but ours, His and mine together.

Before I was called to be the pastor of Pleasant Will Baptist Church, I knew that was where God was going to send me. I was extremely excited to accept the challenges that God had laid before me knowing that my being there was His will for my life at that time.

As I began to pastor, I realized that those who attended Pleasant Will Baptist Church were few, but enthusiastic about doing God's work. I realized that I was not necessarily THE pastor but was A pastor. This body of believers would thrive and only needed a shepherd.

I watched the church continually grow over the years. I saw ministries begin and flourish. Also, I saw ministries I believe to be rejected. Yet, overall, I watched the church steadily grow and extend its boundary without limits to addressing people's spiritual and physical needs as well.

Pleasant Will Baptist Church is a dynamic and flourishing church. The people who attend there have their hearts where they belong. God has blessed them tenfold over the past few years. They have been supportive to every endeavor that I have asked them to support that uplifted God's name. They have generously given of their time, talents, and their treasures. I expect nothing negative to occur because of my leaving as pastor. God is still the head of the church. God's people must still walk by faith. God's people must still pick up their crosses and follow Him.

I have grown greatly by being pastor at Pleasant Will Baptist Church. There were times I know God was pleased with my actions and decisions. There were times I know He was not pleased. As Paul wrote that he prayed faithfully for those who were dear to him (1Cor. 1:4), so do I for those who attend this little church on the hill. My life would never have been complete without my experiences there.

May God richly bless each endeavor there, undertaken for the uplifting of God's name. May He reveal to each of those attending, that He WILL HELP to conquer each challenge that befalls His Church and His people.

I love each of those attending this church with all my heart. May God keep their hearts tender and receptive to the wooing of His Holy Spirit. With continual prayers and thanksgiving, I excitedly encourage each and every one attending Pleasant Will Baptist Church, to continue to go, tell, and baptize in fulfilling the responsibilities required of God's people anchored in God's Church.

THOUGHTS OF A PASSING SHEPHERD

One of the most hallowed truths of life is that God has a plan for each of us and how we are to accomplish this plan during our lives (Jer. 29: 11). Being blessed by being born into a loving Christian family and raised in a God-fearing home environment is of extra value. This instills in us at an early age, a respectful and reverent fear of an omnipotent and omnipresent God (Ps. 69: 5) (Eccl. 12:1). Nurturing godly values from our parents is not optional, but of necessity to help us mature as we grow in Christ. This is especially true if we accept the Lord into our lives at an early age. It is during this time, God's plan and expectations from our lives can sometimes exceed and overwhelm our understanding of His purpose for our lives.

To understand God's touch and purpose for our lives is derived from a basic understanding of His intentions for mankind in general and each of us specifically (Ps. 8:4). God is Holy and Sinless (Isa.53:9). He shows great mercy and forgiveness repeatedly (Pet. 3:9). His promises are sure (2Cor. 1:20). There is nothing that God cannot do. All things are possible with God (Phil. 4:13). God does not NEED us, but we are dead and hopeless WITHOUT Him. Most assuredly, God is the greatest influence in each of our individual lives.

ALL things work to the GOOD to them that love and respect the Lord and are called according to HIS will (Rom. 8:28).

All the above is intended to show to each of my readers that God has an incomparable love for each of us. Through acceptance of Him into our lives, His promises state that obedience to Him will lead to the Windows of Heaven being opened and blessings will be given to us that we will not be able to receive (Mal. 3: 10)!

God's children need to focus on His promises of blessings unimaginable through unlimited power given to His children through the Holy Spirit. Most importantly, with an astute awareness of our enormous inadequacies contrasted by God's immeasurable and incomprehensible forgiveness, we will be less likely to become an ineffective spectator. Knowing this is especially important when we are mindful that the harvest still is great, and the laborers still are few (Matt. 9:37)!

Life with Christ is the most personal and powerful force destined for humanity to guarantee inner peace and stability in a chaotic world. I KNOW that in my life God has in the past and continues with His plan for me. Refusals and even my own resistance often negate His intended blessings especially meant for my life at that time.

As I grew up, He was my protectorate and kept me safe. Through my years of maturation into manhood, He tolerated my rebellious nature and patiently stood by me in times of sorrow when my guilt of disobedience seemed more than I could bear alone. It was for a world such as I, that the plan of Salvation was designed. God Almighty has forgiven my sin through a plan that only He could mastermind, rebuked the power of Satan, and has helped me to stand on solid ground to preach His precious Promises.

God's children who are aware of the above are told to bind together in Christ, pray without ceasing for one another, and especially be mindful of those in great temptations who bear an extra load in the proverbial heat of the day (1Thess. 5: 16-17), (Gal. 6:5).

There are no words imaginable for me to express my gratitude and thankfulness to God Almighty for the ministry that He so graciously and honorably lent to me. However, I would be amiss if I failed to thank the Father for His children that He sent to me, who believing in my ministry, helped undergird this shepherd while feeding the sheep and the lambs.

It should be noted that it is God Himself, alone, who initiates and climaxes each ministry, whether great or small. Any affirmation by the Master's children confirms genuine faith with a rich sense of fellowship from spending time in and around their shepherd's field. To those people who believe that God finishes what He begins in His children's lives (Phil. 1: 6), readers are hereby, urged to remember the Master's warning (Luke 14: 28-29), "for which of you, intending to build (or do anything). . . , sitteth not down first, and counteth the cost, whether he has (what is necessary). . . to finish it? Lest perhaps, after he hath laid the foundation (or started his intentions), and is not able to finish it, all that behold (or see his life), will begin to mock him!"

#1

STORY FOR THE HEART

COME WHAT MAY, I WILL LOVE HIM 'TIL MY DYING DAY

I recently heard a song entitled "Come What May", by Nicole Kidman and Evan McGregor, in which part of the lyrics was "come what may, I will love you 'til my dying day". The loyalty and sacrifice that would accompany such a statement would be most admirable. Yet, that is what Christ said and did, and even more. After His resurrection, He now sits at the right hand of the Father interceding on all Christians' behalf for the wrongs (sins) committed against God. Does it therefore seem expectantly that the Almighty Father would have written, "Let us therefore offer our bodies as a living sacrifice, which is our reasonable service" (Romans 12:1)?

This past week I had the privilege to listen to the Reverend Burke Mohan, pastor of the Road River Baptist Church near Franktown preach a message about the Second Coming of Jesus Christ. He spoke about the similarities among the people's behavior during the days of Noah, Lot in Sodom, and at the anticipated time of Christ's return known as The Rapture of the Church. I was especially interested considering that I had recently preached a similar message during these three different time periods. The Lord, Himself, stated in His Word that in each of these time periods the people were marrying and given in marriage, eating and drinking, buying, selling, planting, building, and other routine life experiences (Luke 17:26-37). What is so wrong and sinful about these activities? In their proper place, probably nothing is wrong. Yet, human nature instills in mankind an insatiable desire to please himself through his own abilities, omitting God from his life.

Israel's greatest king and writer of many psalms, David, wrote, "What is man that You, God, are mindful of him, and that You, God, would send Your Son, Jesus Christ, to die on the Cross of Calvary to redeem him back to the Father (paraphrased Ps. 8:4)? The answer is an unequivocal "for God so loved the world that He gave…" (John 3:16).

God has left nothing out in His plan for mankind. He has given to us at our disposal the abilities to accomplish through Him that which is impossible to the human eye and understanding (Phil. 4:13). The only matter of concern is whether mankind is willing to sacrifice and yield loyalty to God, the Father, to accomplish His goals for our lives. Getting started or restarted with our commitments is not easy to do. However, "Come what may, I will love Him 'til my dying day" is a good way to begin.

#2

STORY FOR THE HEART

WHEN GOD REALLY SPOKE TO A MAN

While I was pastor of Pleasant Will Baptist Church at Walnut, West Virginia, I was also an elementary teacher at Valley Ridge Elementary School in the same community. Hindsight tells me that God had surely smoothed out the wrinkles that would have undoubtedly inhibited my ministry there, relating to preaching to the same people that I would daily discipline favorably or unfavorably their children. Occasionally, I would visit homes throughout the community and often spoke to the people of educational as well as religious subjects.

There was a particular home that I frequented often because of the woman's faithfulness and contributions to church work. I also enjoyed the company of this widowed elderly Christian who often when anticipating my stopping would prepare the most delicious delicacies. It should be noted here that I often mentioned my possible stopping by on a particular day of the week to share some church-related information.

Just across the highway from where this elderly Christian resided, there lived an elderly man who did not attend church, but would periodically walk across the road to enjoy the same delicacies as I. Consequently, there would be times that he and I would both be there simultaneously.

After some initial comments about attending church, he told me that he had gone to the church several years ago that I pastored. He was cordial in receiving my witness but stopped me firmly and politely from time to time if I infringed into unsettling territory as to his relationship with God.

As I returned almost weekly to this household, the woman remarked to me that this elderly gentleman liked me. She added that he felt that I did not pressure him in our conversations. Therefore, when opportunities arose, the more that we talked, the farther I would cautiously delve into his past experiences and apparent abandoning of attending church.

I realized the purpose of my being introduced to this man, after a few months of meeting at this special woman's lunch table. She mentioned to me on one of my visits that he had been diagnosed with cancer, a fast-growing brain tumor. With the now present urgency of this news, I increased my visits, not only to this woman's house, but to his as well. Still yet, he was cordial, but firm when the conversation approached a renewal of the theme of church attendance.

One day while I was there at his house, he openly commented on his years of attending the church on the hill nearby. He told me of an incident happening in one service that I concluded something that the pastor had said aloud, had embarrassed him greatly.

Sadly, he not only left the church on the hill here in Walnut, but after a few months lost his desire to attend any church. He spoke almost broken heartedly as he seemed to lament missing the fellowship over the years of his neighbors at church time. I realized that this man was not saved, and even may have been under conviction of the Holy Spirit and close to a commitment to God at the time that he left. He talked about the church for almost a half an hour while I listened to him. From his conversation I sensed his enjoyment being in church with his friends and neighbors many years back. I surmised that maybe church had been important to his sense of belonging within the community. From his conversation, I concluded that most everyone in this community attended this church.

One day when I stopped to visit him, I found him gone. He had moved to Queen Shed near Clenton. I surprised him when one evening I stopped in to visit. I could tell that the cancer was worsening. The cancer was in his brain and morphine taken was inadequate in dealing with his pain. Although I came back three more times to visit, each time he rejected my attempts at being saved.

As I watched him rock back and forth on the bed suffering intensely with his pain, I told him that I did not know what else to do or say. I pointed out that since he would not listen to me, in desperation I asked, would he listen if God spoke to him?

He stopped rocking for a few seconds and stared at me. Finally, he answered me that yes he would listen to God, if God spoke to him. All I knew to do was drop my head, pray to God, and leave.

Because of his physical condition during my last visit, I suspected that I probably would never see him again, and therefore was surprised when I had an overwhelming desire to go back to see him in a couple of weeks. Immediately, I became positive and suspected that God was sending me back because I might this time lead him to accept Christ as his Savior.

After entering the house, I walked excitedly back into his room where he was again sitting on the bed rocking. His rocking was more intense, and he was speaking profanities with every breath. I did not know what to do. Thinking that I had possibly missed God's intentions for me, I sat down on a chair and remained quiet.

After sitting there for a minute or two with neither of us speaking, he mumbled something aloud that I could not discern. When I asked him what he had said, he remarked in a hostile voice, "I said that He spoke to me!"

I answered back to him, "What did He say?"

After pausing for a moment, he flung a finger at me as if to thrust it through me. He said, "I'll not tell you or anyone else what He said!"

I concluded from his answer that what they had discussed was not to his liking. However, at the same time, I sensed that he was dying to tell me what the One who hangs out the stars, took the time to speak to him said. So, I just sat there quietly.

In a moment or two he shouted out, "I told Him that man didn't have a soul!"

Then I knew what they had discussed. With him saying this, I realized that it was now my turn to speak. I told him about his soul and a loving God, who wanted to forgive us and keep us from going to hell that was not prepared for people, but for Satan and his angels. He still refused to make a commitment for Christ, so I prayed and left.

I learned later that a man driving along the river road stopped at his house and knocked on his door. When allowed inside, he introduced himself as a minister and wondered if someone there needed one. As he visited with this man who was a friend of mine, the minister led my friend to accept Christ into his life.

I have thought often of the Scripture that states, "Sometimes one is to sow the seed, while another may water" (Jn. 4: 37).

I stood in awe at the patience and tolerance that the Lord revealed. I wondered why God had been so tolerant for this man who seemed to only show defiance back to Him. Then I remembered that this man had told a story about how a preacher a long time ago had embarrassed him in a service.

I wondered too, that God had attended the same service long ago that my friend had been embarrassed. Maybe, God, too, regretted the incident and had been waiting to help make amends for a preacher who may have erroneously spoken without thinking about the magnitude of his words; words that were spoken on a beautiful Sunday morning more than 60 years before. Although these words had long been forgotten by probably everyone there that day except my friend, God had heard and remembered them too.

#3

STORY FOR THE HEART

WHAT MANNER OF MAN IS HE? (Mk. 4: 41)

About eight years ago, I owned a brown 2005 Toyota. This was my first Toyota, and I was extremely pleased with it. It exhibited excellent power to travel on the back roads, provided better than average gas mileage on highway and country, and being situated with high suspension gave it a high, off the ground sporty look.

The previous winter had been extremely hard on the West Virginia roadways and several potholes were prevalent by the coming of spring weather. In checking my truck for necessary maintenance, I realized that once again, I need a set of front tires due to the need for a line up.

Brice Cantrell had warned me twice before when I purchased tires for the front, that a line up was necessary. Twice, I had procrastinated in getting the line up done. After wearing out two sets of front tires because I did not get a line up, I stopped in at an auto repair at Wallback for some information regarding lining up the old truck. I was told by one of the mechanics there, that to line up the front end, there were two main bolts on the front axle that needed to be broken loose in order to slide the axle to its proper location. Usually, I was told, that after a couple of years on the road that these bolts would freeze in position and must be cut out. Since my truck was much older than this, the mechanic said that it was obvious that the bolts would need to be cut out and replaced. He added that this was a pretty serious repair and a costly one.

Although I had to have the line up, I was unable to cover the expected cost of the additional estimate. As I left Ferrebee's, my first thoughts were, "I could just hear Brice telling me again. Mike, I have told you twice that you must get that old truck lined up!"

As I left the body shop at Walnut, I started back toward the house up Left Fork Sandy one mile away. As I started driving the old truck back, I began to talk to the Lord. "Lord," I said, "it would be a very small thing for You to do, if You would simply allow these two bolts to break loose so I can get this old truck lined up. However, it would be a Very Big Thing for me if You would."

As I finished my few comments to the Lord, I became aware that I had missed my turnoff for Left Fork Sandy and was descending the back side of Daubens Hill toward the Maysel triangle. Ashamed to go back to Ferrebee's and let them try to break the bolts loose, I drove on over to Dawton's Garage at Two Mile.

As I pulled in front of the garage, the two mechanics came out to greet me and asked how they might help me. I asked them if they had the time to look at my old truck and see what it took to line it up. With no one else waiting for service, I was told to drive on into the garage. I could feel the rush of my heartbeat as both mechanics slapped on hardware to check the condition of the front end. They worked for about five minutes and then each of them stepped backward and stepped out to the front of the truck and looked puzzlingly at each other. At this point I suspected the worst, but tentatively asked, "What is wrong?"

The chief mechanic, James, smiled again and said, "Mike, she's perfectly in line!" I could hardly get to my truck before being overcome with emotions. God had simply decided it was just as easy to line the old truck up as it was to simply break the bolts. I have shared this story with several people, including Brice Cantrell. Lastly, it should be noted that I drove the truck for two more years with neither of the two new front tires showing any wear at all. When I sold the truck, all four tires were as new.

#4

STORY FOR THE HEART

WOMEN IN THE SHADOW OF CHRIST

I was noticing a book that my wife had recently bought entitled, <u>They Were Women Like Me</u>, by Joy Jacobs. As I began to read about the lives of some women who lived during the time of Christ, I could not but wonder about the relationships and difficult emotions that families must have experienced during this time. It seems from reading about these earlier women, that they exhibited strong faith with an unwavering willingness to be in His service, and yet were quite satisfied with ministering in the shadows of sometimes less determined and less faithful men.

The Bible speaks about Martha and Mary who Jesus loved greatly (John 11:5). I wonder how many times the Lord stopped at this household for relaxation and refreshment with His Disciples.

The Book of Mark states that at the cross there were MANY WOMEN present who had followed the Lord and had ministered unto Him (Mark 15:40-41). Although less emphasized by God in His Word than perhaps some men may have been, their qualities of unyielding faithfulness, unmatched courage, and undaunted service to the Lord during a time when women were expected mostly to perform mere menial tasks is clearly noted in Scripture.

At the greatest time in the establishment of the Christian Church, the Resurrection, it was WOMEN who FIRST witnessed the Lord's deliverance from the grave that first Easter morning (Mark 15:9). It was WOMEN who were the FIRST to be given the message I AM ALIVE (Matthew 28:10). It was MEN, however, who were the FIRST to disbelieve the Good News of Christ's Resurrection, although being told previously about it (Matthew 20:19) and were therefore scolded by the Lord for this (Mark 16:14).

When Apostle Paul came into the coast of Philippi, he first preached to women gathered at the riverside (Acts 16:13). There Paul met Lydia, who worshiped God and whose heart the Lord opened. She then led her entire family to Christ, a responsibility normally reserved for the husband (Acts 16:12-15).

When Paul came into the region of Thessalonica to preach Jesus as a suffering Savior, there were MANY WOMEN who believed his message (Acts 17:4). The same situation was repeated at Paul's next location in Berea (Acts 17:12).

In Paul's testimony in Jerusalem to the resistant Jews about his newfound sincerity to Christ, Paul points out that he had beforetime put in prison BOTH MEN AND WOMEN (Acts 22:4).

Many times, when women's involvement in church work is discussed, the quotations of 1 Peter 3:5 which speaks of women being in subjection to their husbands and 1 Corinthians 14:34 which speaks about women being silent in church, are most often the scripture quoted and most remembered by laymen. It should also be mentioned, however, that 1 Corinthians 14:35 states that women are to learn about God and His work for the church FROM THEIR HUSBANDS. Assuredly this was written at a time when husbands were avid readers and doers of God's Word. May God, Himself, intervene on women's behalf when this is no longer the case!

#5

STORY FOR THE HEART

WHERE ARE YOU IN THE CHRISTIANS' OUTREACH OF THE CHURCH?

The Bible, few can dispute, boldly identifies appropriate guidelines to moral and righteous living as desired by God the Father. Jesus said, "as my Father gave me commandment, even so I do (John 14:31). Jesus later encouraged His Disciples to follow His example by saying, "If you love me, keep my commandments" (John 14:15).

In the book of Matthew, Jesus expressed what has often been declared as the Great Commission for Christian responsibility. This is to "go ye therefore, teach all nations, baptizing them in the name of the Father, and of the Son, and of the Holy Ghost" (Matt.28:19). This is a commandment to all Christians and not an option of choice.

To teach and baptize seem to be characteristics relative to bringing new converts into the Church and its fellowship. Jesus also pointed out to His disciples that "I was sick and ye visited me. I was in prison and ye came unto me" (Matt. 25:36). His disciples questioned when they had done this for Him? "When ye have done it unto one of the least of these my brethren, ye have done it unto me" (Matt. 25:40).

What Christian outreach was Jesus making? Was He saying that Christians in church ministries should go and share the Word of God with those who do not personally know Jesus? Was He also suggesting that Christians visit those brethren who are sick or unable to attend church and take God's message to them in outreach ministries? If Jesus meant for His followers to go and witness to those who **will not come** and to those who **can not come**, then what about others who simply **do not come**? Maybe these people are already expected by the Lord to be in God's house partaking in one of the other ministries.

#6

STORY FOR THE HEART

IS GOD'S STILL SMALL VOICE LOUD ENOUGH FOR YOU TO HEAR?

Recently Ranson Schoolcraft, a member of our church and former House of Delegates member and State Senator, had an unfortunate 4-wheeler accident. Without notifying friends or family where he would be riding, Ranson rode off alone into a remote area of Clay County. His 4-wheeler overturned, pinning him underneath for nearly 30 hours. Upon being found after an extensive search, his first comments were" Praise the Lord. He is the only one I've had to talk to."

A rallying rescue troop of 4-wheeler friends and family carefully and quickly transported Ranson to an ambulance where he was taken to Charleston General Hospital. His injuries consisted of a concussion, non-functioning kidneys, severely damaged left arm (that would require amputation just above the elbow), several cuts and bruises, and shock. He later suffered a blood clot in his lungs.

Ranson was sedated due to his injuries for the next week and spent most of the week in a coma state. Slowly, his friends and family could see God answering prayers. His kidneys began functioning and dialysis was discontinued. The body's swelling lessened each day. Cuts began to heal, and bruises began to fade as his awareness began to sharpen and he began to recant his experience. He cried when he spoke about Eron Holton finding him and praised the Lord again. He remarked that he had given up and thought about how his obituary would be read. It was then that he heard Eron's 4-wheeler come along.

The Presbyterian preacher, John Flavel (1630-1691), wrote "Man's extremity is God's opportunity". As I listened to Ranson talk, I could sense he was praising the Lord from the heart. He firmly believed, he said, that God had gotten his attention and given him his life back.

It is true that God continually makes attempts to get our attention. The Bible states that He speaks in a still small voice (I Kings 19:12), through His Word (Mark 12:1, Matt: 4:4), through preachers and teachers (Mark 2:2, Matt. 28:19), and through people's prayers and testimonies (Matt.17:21, Matt. 8:4, Matt. 10:18).

Ranson repeatedly expressed gratefulness for God's mercy and grace since his accident. Clearly Ranson believes if one has a problem hearing God's STILL SMALL VOICE, then God is quite capable of turning the volume up to LOUD AND CLEAR.

#7

STORY FOR THE HEART

COURAGE TO STAND, FOR THAT WHICH IS RIGHT

The Danish writer and musician, Torbin Rick, suggests that to encourage one to change a particular habit creates a resistance based solely upon the need for change itself. This is probably true because life is much like a habit. Most people will agree that it is quite difficult to change a habit, especially one that it takes a lifetime to form.

Even though change is often necessary, human nature resists change by establishing a determined mindset that operates as a survival tactic. Probably words relating to survival tactics said about each of us are less offensive than words like stubborn, bull-headed, or being contrary. Would one agree?

A little over a year ago, having high blood pressure and weighing the most that I had ever weighed, I realized that I was at a crossroads in my life and needed to make a change. My family's health history reflected diabetes, heart problems at an unusually early age, tuberculosis, and Alzheimer's disease scattered throughout its members. I therefore established an attitude of self-survival that included selective eating habits, exercise, disciplining myself at inappropriate eating times, and striving for an optimistic self-esteem that I might live to enjoy life with my family.

When I exercised, I sometimes did so by listening to the country music television station (CMT). As I watched the videos that accompanied the vocals, I noticed a dramatic trend in the number of videos that included American forces and their families as background. This awareness and support of the situations that troops and their families are experiencing today is not uncommon. It does, however, reflect a changed position of many Americans' views when compared to those expressed during the Viet Nam era. Although I did not serve in the armed forces, I did have family members, close friends, and classmates who did serve; some giving their lives. I remember vividly the lack of support many Americans gave to the forces during this conflict. I remember then experiencing disrespect and anger expressed many times directly to the members of our troops.

Seeing this restitution of our country's support to our present troops cannot and will never totally make amends for the past's failure to do so. Assuredly, we can learn from our past mistakes that when we support our people, it does not necessarily mean that we support the cause of the conflict. May this generation be the one who teaches its children more acceptable values of relationships and responsibilities under all circumstances.

Along this same line of thinking, is it not time for many Americans to rethink their position in recognizing and supporting any verbal commitment that they may have made to Jesus Christ?

Our forefathers thought that God was important enough to be the foundation of the establishment of their new nation and they passed this belief firmly to their children. What generations failed to pass it on as firmly? What generation will make amends and get our great country back on its proper foundation? (Acts 4:12)

#8

STORY FOR THE HEART

O, SAY CAN YOU SEE?

When Jesus was preaching on this earth, He quite often quoted Scripture from the Old Testament. In the Gospel of Matthew, Jesus states in Matthew 13:15 (from the Old Testament book of Isaiah) that there are people who hear but do not understand and see but do not perceive. How could this be? Would Jesus be referring to the blinding of their minds rather than the natural blinding of their ears and eyes?

My father has Alzheimer's and there have been times in the past when he would confuse reality with unreality because of the effect of Alzheimer's on his mind and memory. He would periodically relive and mix past experiences causing him at times great frustration as he sought answers.

Is this what Scripture is referring to when it states that the god of this world (Satan) has blinded the minds of them which believe not (in Jesus) lest the light of the glorious gospel of Christ, who is the image of God, should shine unto them (2Cor. 4:4)?

The Bible teaches about Heaven and Hell. In Acts 4:12, Scripture states that there is no other name under Heaven whereby we can be saved but the name of Jesus. Yet Jesus states that people will not come unto Him that they may have life (John 5:40). In this life it is only a disadvantage to be blinded naturally, but truly disastrous to be blinded in our minds about the truth of Jesus Christ in preparation for the next life.

#9

STORY FOR THE HEART

HOW WELL DO YOU KNOW THIS STORY?

As far as I can remember when I was growing up, the movie *The Ten Commandments*, produced and directed in 1923, by Cecil B. DeMille, fascinated me each time that I watched it. I remember that it came on the television every Easter season, and my family watched it faithfully. Now that I have grown older and am preaching, I have some unsettling thoughts regarding the timing of this great epic. As a child growing up, I associated the movie with the season, and therefore the man, Moses, with the central theme of the Easter season. This is not entirely correct.

I also remember that when I was a teacher in 1974 at Christmas time one of my fellow teachers painted the Nativity scene on the door to her classroom. One of her students rushed to me during recess and told me to come with him and look at the Christ child, Moses, painted on his window.

I admit that while I was growing up, my biblical knowledge was shallow at the least. I was quite familiar with stories about the patriarchs as well as the adventurous stories of Biblical heroes. My knowledge and sharing of the *Greatest Story Ever Told*, written by Fulton Oursler, Henry Denker, and James Lee Barrett in 1965 was weak and inadequate to make a lasting impression, however.

God's sheep need to know and be able to share their story about their Shepherd. It may be told in as many ways as there are people telling the story. However, basically, the **story** of Jesus is the foundation of one's Christian faith, and each child of God will stand in judgment for his/her account shared (2Cor. 5:10).

The Bible is God's words (2Tim. 3:16). Its central theme is Jesus Christ from Genesis to Revelation. Yet, the Bible is also God in Word (John 1:1). This is why that when we read His Word that we are in fellowship with God, Himself.

In the first book, Genesis, God creates all that exists. His last and greatest creation is Mankind. Yet, before Genesis ends, mankind disobeys God through the deception of Satan and God destroys mankind except for eight people who He delivers from a catastrophic flood (Gen. 3-10). Mankind's disobedience is termed as SIN and its penalty is determined to be DEATH (Romans 6:23).

However, God provides a Savior for mankind in JESUS CHRIST (John 3:16). Salvation is by God's grace (unmerited favor) through an individual's faith in Christ (Eph.2:8). The newly saved child of God is offered through his/her faith the abundant life (John 10:10), unimaginable favors with God (1Cor. 2:9), protection from Satan (John 10:28), and a future life of eternal bliss with God (1Thess. 4: 13-18), (1Cor. 15:51-58, Chapters 21 and 22 of the Book of Revelations).

Satan, the great deceiver, who is jealous of God and wanted to raise his throne above that of God's in Heaven (Isaiah 14: 12-17) provoked war in Heaven in which one-third of the angelic beings and Satan, himself, were cast out of Heaven to the earth (Rev. 12). Knowing that his time is short before he and his angels are cast into the Lake of Fire (Rev. 20), Satan exerts his wrath for God on God's creation and blinds the minds of people regarding SALVATION THROUGH JESUS CHRIST from an eternal punishment in Hell, a place provided for Satan and his angels (2Cor. 4:3-4).

The **story** about Jesus is so simple that a child can share it, and many do. As we get older, however, we need to modify our account of the story and punctuate it with Scripture to give ourselves credibility. When I was a child, I spoke as a child. I understood it as a child. I thought as a child (1Cor. 13: 11). If one is a young adult or older, maybe it is time to tell the **story** of Jesus with a higher level of validity, backed up and blessed undeniably by God through His Scriptures.

#10

STORY FOR THE HEART

CAN PEOPLE SEE YOUR FATHER IN YOU?

Paul Overstreet sang a hit song in 1990 entitled, *"Seein' My Father In Me"*. When I first heard the song, I thought of my life, and I could not help but think of the ways that I resembled each of my parents. Too, the older that I become, the more that I see of my parents' traits surfacing in my life.

I had not heard the song for some time. It came to mind again, when this past week my younger daughter, Leigh Sarola, walked into a classroom in Richmond, Virginia, as a first-year teacher. She graduated from West Virginia University in 1998 as a Child Life Specialist and has worked the past 5 years in this capacity.

Now, life had taken a different turn. Due to her husband's job opportunity, she and Tadd had been forced to relocate from just outside New York City to their present home in Richmond, Virginia. There, Leigh found herself unemployed. After a few unsatisfying and unsuccessful working experiences, she settled on a teaching opportunity at Heritage High School near Richmond. With 2600 students and 46 new teachers, Leigh walked into this setting this week excited and eager to begin. The day before her first day she called and said, "I believe that I am becoming my parents referring to our long tenure in teaching. This prompted me to once again think of *"Seein' My Father In Me"*.

Before the first day with students, Leigh called me and as she had so often done in her life, asked me to pray for her first day. I was honored to do so.

I thought of King Hezekiah in Second Kings, Chapter 18. The Bible states that he did that which was right in the sight of the Lord (2 Kings 18:3), and that the Lord was with him, and that he prospered whithersoever he went (2 Kings 18:7).

Yet, Sennacherib, King of Assyria, came with a host of 180,000 soldiers to conquer Judah and its capital, Jerusalem (2 Kings 18-19). Because Hezekiah had trusted in the Lord throughout his life, the Lord did not abandon him. The Lord sent the prophet, Isaiah, to tell Hezekiah that the Assyrians "shall not come into this city, nor shoot an arrow there, nor come before it with shield, nor cast a bank against it" (2 Kings 19:32). Regarding the great host of Assyrians, one angel walked through their camp during the night and when morning came, all were dead (2nd Kings 19:35).

I have watched my daughter grow in the Lord her 28 quickly passing years. I know how meaningful that a relationship with Jesus Christ is for her. I am proud of her in so many ways, but especially that I *am "seein' my heavenly Father in her"*.

#11

STORY FOR THE HEART

HOW GREAT IS YOUR FAITH?

The Bible speaks of God showing His children MYSTERIES (1Cor. 15: 51) and hiding His people in SECRET PLACES (Psalms 31: 20). Agreeably, the Bible is a difficult book to read and understand if one is NOT seeking to find God's truths (Matt. 7: 7) and is NOT expecting the Lord God to OPEN his UNDERSTANDING of what is being read (Matt. 16: 17).

The most profound and basic truth that the Bible presents is that man is a sinner who has disobeyed God and is deserving of death (Romans 6: 23). However, in the same verse that pronounces death on humanity, an opportunity for life is provided. Salvation is not only the NEW beginning of one's life in Christ, but it introduces an individual to the only possible way of understanding and developing a relationship with an omnipotent, omnipresent, all-seeing God through the avenue of faith (Ephesians 2: 8), (Hebrews (11: 6).

The Bible speaks of LITTLE faith and GREAT faith. The Bible states that faith is imperative to pleasing the Lord (Hebrews 11: 6).

Is it not, therefore, understandable that Christians should desire to acquire GREAT faith?

In Matthew chapter 8, there is an account of a LEPER coming to Jesus for healing. This account is followed by one about a CENTURION who is asking the Lord to heal his servant. In these two accounts one can understand the importance of faith.

In chapters 5-7 the Lord had been preaching to multitudes of people in what is commonly known as the Sermon on the Mount. He ended His preaching and retreated to the mountain to be alone. When He came down from the mountain, the multitude sought Him out and SO DID A LEPER. The leper said to the Lord, "Lord, if thou wilt, thou canst make me clean" (Matt. 8: 2). WHERE did the leper get the faith to believe that the Lord could heal him? It should be noted that one DOES NOT RECEIVE faith from the OBSERVATION of MIRACLES, but that FAITH COMETH FROM HEARING THE WORD OF GOD (Romans 10: 17). Does this indicate that the leper had heard the Master preach BEFORE this encounter? Absolutely! Also, if he had faith then, why wasn't he healed then? Relatively speaking, when people hear the Word of God preached and believe it, are they then saved? Not always! One of Satan's greatest weapons is fear (2 Tim. 1-7). The leper was an outcast in society and excluded from public contact. Therefore, his fear is understandable. What is to be FEARED by PEOPLE TODAY who hear the Word of God preached, but then fail to act upon the invitation to accept Christ as Lord and Savior?

In the second example the CENTURION made a request to the Lord to heal his servant of palsy. The Lord offered to go with him to his house, but the centurion simply asked the Lord to "speak the word only and my servant shall be healed." (Matt 8: 8). The Lord complimented the centurion's GREAT faith. Where did he get this great faith? He, too, had undoubtedly heard the Lord preach before this encounter. However, unlike the leper, the centurion HAD undoubtedly ACCEPTED THE LORD'S INVITATION THEN to believe in Christ. He most likely, too, had gone several times when the opportunity provided him to hear the Lord preach again and therefore had his faith strengthened.

In contrasting these two individuals, the leper, and the centurion, we surely can derive that each had a problem and believed that the Lord could meet his needs. Each based his belief on former preaching heard of the Lord. The centurion's faith was said to be greater than any other faith seen in all Israel (Matt. 8: 10). Can we infer that to attain strong faith to help others meet their needs in Christ, we must spend more time in communion with God (1Thess. 5: 16-18), (James 5: 16)?

Lastly, the LEPER was told "see thou tell no man", while the CENTURION was simply told to "go thy way; and as thou hast believed, so be it done unto thee" (Matt. 8: 13). Was the leper told to avoid contact with unbelievers who would surely discourage him before he got to the temple (church) and had his testimony strengthened? Was the centurion's testimony strong enough to handle scoffers?

WHO ARE WE MOST LIKE, the leper or centurion? Is our faith only strong enough to ask God to HELP US? Do other people discourage our testimony?

We do not know the impact that either of these two individuals had on the people around them. We do know that one got a later start than the other. STARTING LATER IN LIFE, HOWEVER, IS BETTER THAN NEVER STARTING AT ALL.

#12

STORY FOR THE HEART

ARE YOU ONE OF THE HARVEST OR ONE OF THE LABORERS?

As the year 2005 ends, I am sure that the memories of the past year are filled with mixed emotions. The passing of time has brought about the passing of some people who were very dear to us. However, Apostle Paul reminded us of whatsoever things that had virtue or praise for our Heavenly Father we were to think on these things (Phil. 4:8). In so doing, each of us would become better prepared to meet our Heavenly Father as we continued our daily Christian living.

Christmas Day occurred on a Sunday this year and this hopefully helped each one present in the service to personally relate to the story and message of Christmas. The **story** of Christmas is about a young babe born in a manger long ago in Bethlehem (Luke 2). His name was Jesus, God's Son, who is the Savior of all humanity. The **message** of Christmas is somewhat deeper, but so simply revealed in Scripture. The message of Christmas is the repeated message throughout the Bible; God speaks, and mankind responds (Jn. 3: 16).

Throughout the Scriptures, God has spoken IN different ways and THROUGH different individuals. In the Old Testament God, Himself, spoke to the prophets, and they in turn, spoke God's messages to others.

In the New Testament, God, the Father, spoke to mankind through His Son, Jesus, and the Holy Spirit. He has also spoken through His Disciples and Apostles, as well as the Word of God itself. Mankind's obligation is to respond to God's speaking.

In responding to God's speaking, mankind either answers yes or no to God's seeking him to go, take, help, come, give, teach, preach, or countless other requests. Regrettably, mankind has in latter years responded to God with a third choice, no answer at all! Somehow, this seems to imply that although one is NOT saying yes, he is NOT saying no! Would this answer fall into the category of the Laodiceans (Rev. 3:14-15)?

In Luke, chapter 2, God speaks through an angel. First, the angel stated, "I bring you good tidings of great joy, which shall be to all people." Does not every messenger of God today share the same sentiments to his/her audience? Secondly, the angel stated, "For unto you is born this day in the city of David a Savior, which is Christ the Lord." This is also the message that God's people share with others. Thirdly, the angel stated, "Ye shall find the babe wrapped in swaddling clothes, lying in a manger."

Is it not logical that if God speaks about His Son, then He would tell mankind where His Son could be found? The Scripture states that "seek and thou shall find; knock and it shall be opened unto you" (Matt. 7:7). Is there anyplace that Jesus could not be found if one were sincerely looking for Him? Therefore, the message of Christmas is a repetition of the central theme of the Bible!

Notice the response of the shepherds to God's speaking through the angel. First, "Let us now go even unto Bethlehem, and see this thing which is come to pass, which the Lord hath made known unto us" (Luke 2: 15). Is this not a fitting response of everyone who needs to come to Christ to see for himself/herself if Jesus is really who Christians say that He is?

Secondly, "and when they had seen it, they made known abroad the saying which was told them concerning this child" (Luke 2: 17-19). Is this saying that the shepherds BELIEVED and TESTIFIED the statement of the angel? Is this not what Christians are expected to testify themselves?

Thirdly, the shepherds "returned, glorifying and praising God for all the things that they had heard and seen, as it was told unto them" (Luke 2: 20). Does this not simply say that the shepherds CAME TO SEE for themselves, BELIEVED in the Christ, and CONTINUED living their lives GLORIFYING and PRAISING God with their TESTIMONIES?

Those people who have never asked God to save them through the Savior of all mankind, JESUS, need to come to Him to see if He really is who the Bible says that He is! Christians, too, need to come to Jesus AGAIN and AGAIN to see what He has for them to do to help get the message of Christmas and the Bible "to all people" (Luke 2: 10). Once this occurs, the harvest which Jesus said, "is plenteous" just might be reduced as "the labourers which Jesus said were few" (Matt. 9: 37), receive an increase!

#13

STORY FOR THE HEART

THE LONGER WE WAIT, THE GREATER THE COST

    The books of the Bible, Luke and Acts, were both written by the Gentile physician Luke to Theophilus, that he "mightest know the certainty of those things wherein thou have been instructed (Luke 1:4)." It seems, therefore, that Theophilus had been introduced to Jesus Christ and probably was already a Christian. However, Luke may have wanted his Christian brother to be absolutely certain of his belief because to know assuredly is the basis of one's faith (I John 4:7, 13), (1 John 5:13, 19).

    Luke most likely received his information from traveling with Apostle Paul, according to the second century writer, Irenaeus, bishop of Lyons. His purpose for writing Acts was to encourage the reader's faith. Luke's noting that each individual's need to continue steadfastly in the doctrine of Jesus Christ, fellowship one with another regularly, participate in the Lord's Supper service, and continually practice sincere prayer habits (Luke 2:42) are all consistent with Apostle Paul's instruction to the churches of Asia Minor that he helped establish.

The Book of Acts lays the foundation for successful church ministry as evident by the miracles the Disciples performed and the rapid growth of the body of believers. Christians today can learn much from the compassion and courage these undaunted soldiers for Jesus Christ exhibited. Learning the success story of the early Christian churches should provide today's believers with valuable insight to overcoming Satan's attempts to hinder church growth. Read this exciting book again and envision oneself in first century Palestine traveling with Apostle Peter or Apostle Paul.

Consider the rejections and the many threats of intimidation leveled toward the early disciples from nonbelievers. Then and only then, evaluate whether witnessing for Jesus Christ is as difficult or dangerous today as it certainly was 2000 years ago.

We need to be most mindful that we may be living in the least obtrusive time in history for sharing the Word of God to a lost and dying world. Therefore, we should be more tolerable and be less offended toward those who reflect their disapproval of our witness. Irregardless, it is certain that the disapproval that these individuals show toward us for witnessing to them is by far less than the disapproval that the Lord God of the universe will show toward us, if we DO NOT!

#14

STORY FOR THE HEART

ARE YOU GOING, TELLING, BAPTIZING, OR JUST FISHING?

Jesus Christ lived upon this earth some thirty years. Yet undeniably His presence THEN and TODAY continues to change people's lives. He said that He came to "do His Father's will, (John. 5: 30) which was to SEEK and SAVE people who were LOST WITHOUT JESUS (Luke 19: 10). His life was to be an example as He said, "Follow Me" (John. 21: 19). His last commission to His followers was to "go, teach, and baptize others who seek Him (Matt. 28: 19). How many Christians TODAY seriously consider THIS commission as OUR commission and view ourselves as SOUL WINNERS?

Why do some people NOT view themselves as SOUL WINNERS? In the Gospel of Matthew, one MAY FIND some answers. In Matthew, chapter 26, Jesus spent the evening with His Disciples. He ate the PASSOVER meal, WASHED His Disciples' FEET, and initiated COMMUNION. He had FULFILLED the LAW, exemplified HUMILITY as being imperative, and gave

EACH of them work to do. Then He stunned them by saying that before the night would end, each of them would abandon Him destined for the CROSS. Above all the others, PETER vehemently denied his forsaking of his loyalty to the Lord. The Lord answered Peter's statement with "That this night, before the cock crow, thou shalt deny me THRICE" (Matt. 26: 34)! Sadly, Peter did.

After His resurrection, Christ appeared unto His Disciples three times (John. 20: 19), (John. 20: 26), and (John. 21: 4). Although Jesus had specifically instructed His Disciples to "go, remit, or retain people's sins" (John. 20: 23), at this third appearance, Jesus finds them FISHING (John. 21: 3)!

Peter's actions THEN were much like ours TODAY. First, Peter was trying to re-establish PEACE with GOD by sharing time with friends. Unfortunately, FRIENDS CANNOT MEND what is BROKEN BETWEEN ONE AND GOD. Secondly, Peter sought satisfaction for himself by retreating into the past where situations were more familiar, and outcomes were more predictable. This excludes a REQUIRED WALK BY FAITH (Heb. 11: 6) and is doomed to fail. Lastly, Peter (as well as the others) had been given work to do by the Lord which had been ignored.

Peter, HOWEVER, did rectify his wrongs. After the miraculous catch of fish which Jesus gave them, the Disciples were asked by Jesus to come to Him. PETER DID SO. When the Disciples each had come to Jesus, He asked Peter if he, Peter, loved Him more that these other THINGS first thought to be important. Peter DID NOT say, "Why don't YOU, LORD, ask one of the other Disciples if HE loves YOU?" Peter's answer implied that his remembrance of the

Disciples' denial was focused solely UPON HIS DENIAL. Boldly, Peter answered affirmatively three times IN THE PRESENCE OF THE OTHERS that he loved the Lord wholeheartedly.

The three mistakes made by Peter are often made by many Christians today. To avoid the responsibility of "soul winning", God's people sometimes attempt to find peace with God through family, friends, or work, but to no avail. They will even retreat to the safety of the past with familiar settings and situations. Either of these leads to an unanswered call to God's will.

Peter, however, learned from his mistakes. So should we. Peter CAME TO JESUS when He called. So should we. Peter placed his denial, his sin, foremost in his mind. So should we. Peter then testified to the Lord in the presence of others. So should we. Too many Christians testify too few times.

The last words that Jesus spoke to His followers were "go, teach, and (after God convicts and saves) then baptize" (Matt. 28: 19). The harvest is still white, and the laborers are still too few (Luke 10: 2). Jesus said that He gave unto His followers "the keys to the Kingdom of Heaven" (Matt.16: 19). What a tremendous treasure for God's children to have in their possession! If we have made the mistakes that Peter made, let them remain in the PAST. It is NOW our time to follow Peter's lead and make situations right in our own lives and in those lives of our loved ones we cherish enough to spend an eternity with, in Heaven. Let us TODAY become a SOUL WINNER!

#15

STORY FOR THE HEART

MAY YOUR DREAMS COME TRUE

Certainly, everyone dreams and wishes that some of these dreams come true. Are dreams just wishful memories or is there biblical support to believe that our dreams may come true?

In 1 Kings 3: 5, the Bible states that God appeared unto Solomon, David's son, and newly chosen King of Israel, in a dream at night. In this subconscious state of mind, Solomon is given a wish from God. Solomon answers first by speaking humbly about his father, David, and how God has blessed David's kingship solely because of his obedience to God (1Kings 3: 6). Solomon then reflects upon his own inadequacy to succeed his father (1Kings 3: 7). Weighing all matters quite responsibly, Solomon asked God for an understanding heart to judge His people fairly and compassionately (1Kings 3: 9). Because Solomon had asked unselfishly placing God's best interest foremost, God granted his wish and added blessings of riches and honor from the people.

If Solomon's dream came true, is there a possibility that ours may also? Solomon acknowledged his godly teaching and others' influence upon his life (1Kings 3: 6). So should we. Solomon acknowledged his inability to succeed without God's assistance (1Kings 3: 7-8). So should we. Solomon's wish centered upon pleasing God (1Kings 3: 9). So should ours. Lastly, Solomon believed and followed his dream (1Kings 3: 15). So should we.

Not all dreams may reflect God speaking to us. Some may not even make sense at all! The Bible states, however, that God speaks to His children in the still small voice (1Kings 19: 12). As sometimes the clutter of other voices and interference tend to distract us, we certainly can be certain when we hear God's voice. So must we sort through our many dreams knowing God's will for each of us. Since we are the apple of His eye (Deut.32: 10), should there be any doubt that God's greatest desire is to make our dreams come true?

#16

STORY FOR THE HEART

WHAT IS THE FOCUS OF OUR FAITH?

The Bible teaches that Jesus Christ was born of a virgin, lived a sinless life, and died on the Cross at Calvary for the sins of the whole world (Matt.1) (Luke 23). It also teaches that Jesus was resurrected from the dead after three days, ascended back to heaven, and now sits at the right hand of the heavenly Father making intercessions for those people who have Him as their Savior and Lord (Luke 24) (Heb.7). The Bible further points out this same Jesus is coming again to establish an everlasting kingdom with His believers who have died (1Thess. 4: 13-18), as well as those who will be alive at the time of His return (Jn. 14).

With this belief as the focus of the Christian faith, it is the responsibility of each believer to herald this news to a lost and dying world of unbelievers. Jesus' last words to His Disciples reiterated this common theme recorded throughout the Gospels (Matt. 28: 18-20). How is the church succeeding in this endeavor to save the world from a devil's hell (Matt. 25: 41)?

Often, any church's shortcomings fall on the messenger and not with the message. This is probably true whether the messenger is a preacher or a lay spokesperson. It is most assuredly true that Satan can more easily amplify faults with man rather than with God. To be a spokesperson for God is an awesome responsibility to undertake, at any level. One needs to realize that the power to convert people lies entirely with the message. Knowing this, it may be only necessary to fine tune messengers rather than overhaul messages!

In the book of Numbers, God told Moses to "SEND thou men, that they may SEARCH the land of Canaan, which I GIVE unto the children of Israel. Of every tribe of their fathers shall ye send a man, everyone a RULER among them" (Num. 13: 2). Moses followed the Lord's command by sending the men as spies into the land of Canaan to "SEE the land, what it is and the people that dwelleth therein (Num. 13: 17-18).

Did Moses ADD to God's request by mentioning to the spies to see if the people were STRONG or WEAK. . . FEW or MANY and lived in TENTS or STRONG HOLDS for homes? They were to see if the land were GOOD or BAD . . . FAT OR LEAN also (Num. 13: 18-20). Is it often true that when people are told to look for good or bad points that they will find BOTH! If God had CHOSEN this land as a GIFT to the children of Israel, did Moses inadvertently instill doubt in some of the men's minds of Canaan's value?

The men searched the entire land from Kadeshbarnea in the south to Hamath in the north. Upon returning after 40 days, ten of the twelve men only had ONE POSITIVE comment to make. This was that the land was truly a "land flowing with milk and honey"

(Num. 13: 27). That one positive comment, however, was overwhelmingly outweighed by the MANY NEGATIVES mentioned by the ten! Is it often true that FEARFUL men are often FAITHLESS ones also? Was this further substantiated by their statement that ALL THE PEOPLE THAT WE SAW IN IT ARE MEN OF GREAT SIZE (Num. 13: 32)? Yet the only giants were those sons of Anak located near Hebron.

Of all the places the spies passed through, only Hebron was mentioned. Was this city the expected high point of their journey through the land because it was the burial place of their ancestors Abraham and his wife, Sarah? It was also the burial location of Isaac and Rebekah as well as Jacob and Leah (Gen.49: 29-31). Is it not true that if our faith is centered upon a PLACE, PERSON, or THING and not upon JESUS CHRIST, then Satan has an avenue to attack us? Was it coincidental that the sons of Anak, the giants, also lived near Hebron, Israel's most highly respected memorial in Canaan?

The ending result of the mission was that ten out of twelve spies brought a discouraging report which caused the people to weep all night (Num. 14: 1). The negative report discouraged the people to the point that they wanted to return to Egypt (Num. 14: 4) from which they had so recently and joyfully exited. The outcome for the people was that their disbelief and rejection of God's intentions for them, destined the entire body to spend the next 40 years eating manna and quail in the wilderness.

When 40 years had passed, only Caleb, Joshua, and those who had been under the age of twenty, 40 years earlier, entered God's

Promised Land. When Israel entered Canaan, Caleb repeated his request to conquer the giants as he vowed 40 years earlier to Moses.

Could it be probable that the pitfalls that befell the Israelites may sometimes be the ones that hinder the work of the present-day church? FIRST, when God's children (both preachers and lay persons) are asked to give a message to a group or to one individual, messages need to be given as they are received. SECONDLY, if one's faith is centered upon a building, a special place, or a specific person, that faith is in vain and is easily challenged by Satan. THIRDLY, people who are afraid exercise little or no faith. Fear is not of God (2Tim. 1: 7).

Caleb's faith was as strong 45 years later as it had been earlier in his life. Although the circumstances of life often teach us to gain and progress as we grow older, faith is not as such. Faith comes by hearing the Word of God (Romans 10:17). By continually reading and listening to the Word of God, God's people should acquire great faith and maintain that faith throughout their lives. God's people today need not wait 40 years to exercise their faith. There are always mountains to climb and giants to conquer. God was waiting patiently for the children of Israel to make their decision THERE IN THE WILDERNESS. He is waiting just as patiently for you and me to make our decisions HERE IN OUR LIVES today about going forward or standing still. As in the case in the wilderness where the destiny of countless lives was decided by just a few people, so is there today in the church where the harvest truly is plenteous, but the laborers are still few (Matt. 9: 37).

#17

STORY FOR THE HEART

A LIFE AS AN OPEN BOOK

The Psalmist, David, was one of the most colorful characters in the Bible. His life is basically an open book covering from the time that he was a shepherd boy in the hills of Judea (1Sam. 16) to his last words as King of Israel (1Kings 1) (2 Sam. 23). Focusing on just one part of David's life such as his victory over Goliath or his sin with Bathsheba would not give David justice in evaluating his relationship with God and God's purpose for sharing David's life with humanity.

David was a man of passion as evident throughout his life. God placed him as King of Israel when Saul, Israel's first king, was rejected. The prophet, Samuel, told Saul that he was being rejected and that God had sought Himself a man after His own heart (1Sam. 13:14). This became evident as David expressed his great love for the Lord in the writing of his psalms, his constant calling upon the Lord for guidance and forgiveness in his reign, and his desire to build the Lord a magnificent temple.

David was not, however, a man who made no mistakes. Besides his sin with Bathsheba which he responded with Psalms 51, his vanity and pride would cost thousands of lives when he wanted to know the extent of HIS kingdom (1Chron. 21). Yet, even in this costly mistake, David responded to God that it wasn't the sheep's fault (meaning the people), but that it was his fault. He then asked God to punish him and not the people for his mistake (1Chron. 21: 17).

David's passion is realized in numerous places in Scripture. Realizing that passion is having a great desire to accomplish an endeavor with great energy, a reader needs to remind himself not to assume that David's passion for people overshadowed his passion for God.

When David wrote Psalms 23, he gave to the Scriptures a most treasured writing. Beginning with the words, "the Lord is my Shepherd" and concluding with "and I will dwell in the house of the Lord forever" gives its reader not only a PLACE of comfort but also its DURATION. The words, "I shall not want" reflect in David a change from that which he had wanted . . . from HIS desires to God's. His thought that God "MAKETH him to lie down in green pastures" infers that David MAY have needed some coaxing in this matter. It should be noted that the "leading beside the still waters, restoring his soul, and being led in the paths of righteousness" all prepared him for the "walk through the valley of the shadow of death".

God continually tries to change His people's "wants" so that they may be led to STILL waters in a TURBULENT, UNFORGIVING world. It is in these still waters that He restores our souls and prepares us for the valley ahead (Heb.9: 27).

Scripture states, "Be still and know that I am God "(Ps.46: 10). Most importantly, let us realize that the faith that we bring TO the valley is the ONLY faith that will help take us THROUGH this valley. Remembering that faith comes ONLY from hearing the WORD OF GOD (Rom.10: 17), let us be more attentive to God's preparation for our lives in asking God to open the Scriptures for our understanding.

Everything in life is secondary when we find ourselves in the valley of the shadow of death. MANY people for MANY different reasons come THROUGH this valley MANY times. However, ALL people will surely come TO this valley at least one time. David said, "Yea, though I walk THROUGH the valley of the shadow of death, I WILL FEAR NO EVIL, for THOU ART WITH ME". This statement of AFFIRMATION reflected his CONFIRMATION of his GREAT faith in the Lord that he exercised from the time of his rule over a few sheep in the hills of Judea to the time of his reign over many sheep as God's king of Israel.

#18

STORY FOR THE HEART

ATTRIBUTES OF A LOVING SAVIOR

Recently I preached the 18th chapter of Genesis which focuses on an encounter between Abraham and the Lord God in the plains of Mamre in Hebron. As I studied this chapter, I wondered if hidden within this encounter between the Lord God and two angels with Abraham and Sarah, were there underlying characteristics for Christian living today that could be seen in Abraham's relationship with the Lord God then? Certainly, Christians search the Bible for guidelines to successful living as promised by Jesus Christ, Himself (Jn. 10: 10), and this passage may well be one of many such guidelines.

First as the Lord and the two angels approached Abraham, Abraham recognized the Lord God. This is noted by Abraham's addressing Him as "My Lord" and I am "thy servant" (Gen. 18: 3). It is further supported by Abraham's acknowledgement of the Lord as the "Judge of all the earth" (Gen. 18: 25). The inference here is that God's people should recognize God's voice when spoken to them.

His children should be recognized as they exercise their ministries of preaching, teaching, singing, or other gifts.

Secondly, Abraham showed hospitality and respect to the Lord and His companions by giving them cool water to drink, washing their feet, and feeding them bread, cakes, and fresh cooked veal with butter and milk (Gen. 18: 4-8). This reflected a sense of respect and courtesy for God's servants. It does not indicate that one is to give any more than what is needed for refreshment and sustenance.

Thirdly, the Lord announced to Abraham and Sarah that they would have a child in the next few months (Gen. 18: 9-15). This was quite difficult for them to accept because of their respective ages of 100 and 90 years old. The Lord countered with the statement, "Is anything too hard for the Lord" (Gen. 18: 14)?

Certainly, Scripture substantiates that Christ has all power given to Him in Heaven and earth (Matt. 28: 18). He related to His Disciples the last night with them that they would do "greater works than the ones He had done" (Jn. 14:12). As He sent them out to witness of Him, He gave them "power to tread on serpents and scorpions, and over the power of the enemy and nothing by any means would hurt them" (Luke 10: 19). Paul would later acknowledge that he could do "all things through Christ which strengtheneth me" (Phil. 4: 13). Christians today have access to this same power through Christ, do they not?

In Genesis 18: 17, the Lord discussed sharing His intentions relating to Sodom. The purpose of this was to inform Abraham that his nephew, Lot, who lived there was in danger. Does God not warn His children about their friends and family who are in danger? Are

Christians not encouraged to warn others about the reality of Hell? Does not Christ's commission to His children suggest urgency in their witnessing?

As Christians stand and testify in churches and countless other places about their Lord and Savior, they testify of His salvation and accompanying blessings. However, in Genesis 18: 18-19, the Lord testifies to the angels with him about Abraham! Can we draw the conclusion that when we lift up the Lord Jesus, that He lifts us up in the eyes of others to give credibility to our witness and ministries?

In verses 20 unto the end of the chapter, the Lord discusses Sodom's fate. Interceding for Lot, Abraham discusses the righteous being destroyed with the ungodly. Quite obviously the Lord's patience is shown as Abraham considers the number of righteous needing to be present within the city to spare its destruction. Is there a Christian who cannot testify repeatedly of the Lord's tolerance and patience with him or her?

Lastly, it is noted that Sodom is destroyed, but Lot is spared. Too often, God's children find themselves, as Lot did, in the wrong place at the wrong time. God, however, is a faithful God. Therefore, at these times, the righteous through Jesus Christ will be saved, but they may, as Lot learned, suffer great loss.

#19

STORY FOR THE HEART

A LESSON OF HUMILITY

There are many concepts and fundamental principles the Lord tries to teach His children through different avenues. One would hardly consider picking up litter along the highway as an instructional avenue for Him to use in teaching people appropriate Christian values. Yet, I have found this to be true in my life.

In the last two years the Pleasant Will Baptist Church has worked in connection with the West Virginia Department of Highways and Ivywell Elementary School to help control litter along the highway from Clayton unto Ivywell. It was hoped that this project would be one that would not only help beautify our highway but also teach children to be more responsible when discarding litter.

It might be assumed that the focus of this Pastor Point would be on the HABITS OF THE PEOPLE WHO DISCARD LITTER. That is not the focal point of this writing. There have been three important concepts that I, myself, have learned from PICKING UP THE LITTER.

My procedure of picking up litter included walking, riding a bicycle, and riding in a vehicle. The mode of travel depended upon the amount of litter to be collected. Also, to help to control the amount of litter being discarded, the church had installed six PLEASE HELP KEEP CLEAN signs along this eleven-mile distance. Educational presentations continued to be given to the Ivywell School children so that those who traveled the road most frequently were reminded. Regrettably, those who discarded refuse improperly continued to do so. When the program started, I remember thinking that people would be most appreciative for a REPEATED effort to maintain the roadway and that litter would surely cease along this eleven-mile highway. This has not been the case. Although litter amounts have certainly decreased, it seems that some people's bad habits are still very hard to break.

FIRST OF ALL, I have an increased TOLERANCE toward others. The Lord has encouraged me in this area of growth by allowing me to focus on His tolerance toward me. I continue bad habits and as Apostle Paul said it so eloquently, "For that which I do I allow not: for what I would, that do I not; but what I hate, that do I." (Romans 7: 15). I ask the Lord daily for His forgiveness and have experienced firsthand the Lord's sincere effort to teach people to live more harmoniously.

SECONDLY, to be appropriately equipped to pick up litter, one needs to be dressed for high visual identification, wear rubber gloves to handle a variety of unclean refuse and carry several orange litter bags that give passer-bys warning that road work is in progress. Certainly, I have learned HUMILITY by being dressed in blaze orange, carrying orange garbage bags, and picking up such items as dirty diapers, men's spit containers, partially filled alcohol containers that often spill onto my clothing, and countless other bits of foul and filth.

THIRDLY, besides tolerance and humility, God has most importantly taught me about LOVE. In 1 Corinthians, chapter 13, the Lord tells us through Paul's writing that LOVE IS THE GREATEST GIFT to possess. I must admit that when people repeatedly discard refuse while knowing that the highway has just been cleaned is sometimes frustrating. Am I saying that God has taught me to have a great love toward these people who discard refuse improperly? No. However, I love them more than I once did!

#20

STORY FOR THE HEART

HOW SKILLED ARE YOU WITH YOUR SWORD?

Through the inspiration of God (2 Tim. 3: 16), the psalmist wrote, "What is man, that THOU are mindful of him" (Psalms 8: 4)? What were God's intentions for creating mankind as the masterpiece of His creative process?

In Genesis 1:26, the Scripture declares God's words, "Let Us make man in Our image, after Our likeness:" After doing so, God further gave dominion to the man over the fish of the sea and over the fowl of the air, and over the cattle, and over ALL the earth, and over every creeping thing that creepeth upon the earth (Gen.1:26). God saw ALL that He had created and declared that it was GOOD (Gen. 1:31). God continued to bless the man by planting a garden eastward in Eden and put man and woman there to take care of it (Gen. 2:8). God still honored man by allowing him to give a name to all that He, Himself, had created (Gen.2:19).

It would become clear, as God came to Adam there in the garden (Gen. 3:8), that God desired to fellowship and bless the man and woman with His presence and blessings (Gen. 2:9). When mankind would reject God's fellowship, God declared an almost total annihilation of His creation. Only one family, Noah, his wife, three sons and their wives was spared as Noah found GRACE in God's eyes (Gen. 6:8).

As mankind continued to reject God's fellowship, God drew to Him those who would seek Him (Gen. 12: 1-7). Scripture repeatedly declares that God wants to bless those He has drawn to Himself, (John 10:10), for where there is instruction and fellowship with God, there is WORSHIP of GOD (Gen. 24: 48).

The Book of Psalms is probably the most filled praise book in the Bible. In closing the Book, the psalmist declares that God's people are to sing a "NEW SONG" (Psa.96). In Revelations 5, the subject of this new song is "the WORTHINESS OF JESUS CHRIST"!

Is it not understandable to us for God, who has given ALL, should expect man, who has given SO LITTLE, to have respect and praise for HIS SON, JESUS CHRIST? The psalmist declares that this new song is to be shared PUBLICLY (Psalms 149: 1) (Psalms. 96: 1). Also, in this Psalms the writer states that the Lord TAKETH PLEASURE in His people (Psalms 149: 4). If He takes pleasure in His people, who are MOST UNWORTHY, then would it not seem logical for us to take GREAT PLEASURE in Him who is MOST WORTHY? Through the Psalmist, God relates to His children tremendous potential to enjoy the victorious life through JESUS CHRIST (Psalms 149: 6-10).

The Christian needs only HIGH PRAISES OF GOD (testimony) in his/her mouth and a two-edged sword, the Bible

(Rev.1: 16) in his/her hand to fulfill his/her purpose for their lives (Psalms 149: 6).

Bibles can easily be purchased and are relatively inexpensive. One's TESTIMONY, however, costs an individual somewhat more!

#21

STORY FOR THE HEART

HOW WAS YOUR HARVEST THIS YEAR?

In Luke 12: 13-15, there is a story about a man who approaches Jesus with a question regarding his inheritance. It appears that the man's brother had been given the responsibility of dividing the inheritance between the two and he had not done so properly. By Jesus failing to intervene into the matter AND by speaking the word "covetousness" to the young man, Jesus exposes the brother's motive to acquire more inheritance than his share.

To further help His Disciples understand the concept of coveting to satisfy one's needs, Jesus spoke to them a parable. The parable was the story of a rich man whose ground brought forth plentifully. Not knowing exactly what to do with the excessive blessings bestowed upon him, the man decided to tear down his barns and build new ones. This would allow him to enjoy a life of ease for many years. The LORD SAID THE MAN WAS A FOOL FOR LAYING UP TREASURES FOR HIMSELF AND WAS NOT RICH TOWARD GOD (Luke 12: 21).

On the surface, as in the case with the man seeking help with his inheritance, this rich man seemed sincere in his efforts to avoid wasting any blessings given him. Most certainly, there isn't anything wrong with being blessed with more than is needed. Unfortunately, the man made some erroneous conclusions. **First** his being blessed ABOVE his capacity to receive CAUSED HIM FRUSTRATION (What shall I do, because I have no room to bestow my fruits?) (Luke 12: 17).

Secondly, he declared that ALL that he had raised was HIS! (MY fruits, MY barns, MY goods) (Luke 12: 18). In Hosea 2:8-9, God tells Hosea to tell His people that the corn, wine, oil, wool, and flax (used in retrieving linseed oil and the stalk for making linen) were HIS. **Thirdly**, if THIS YEAR his barns were TOO SMALL, might it be possible that NEXT YEAR they might be TOO LARGE? Anticipation of continuing circumstances including blessings is NOT biblical without God's approval (Prov.27: 1). **Fourthly**, this foolish man was hoarding his treasures for the world that he was rapidly LEAVING and ignoring preparation for the world that he was rapidly GOING TO BE ENTERING! **Lastly**, the rich man's goal was to arrive at a place in his life where he would not have to WORK. Jesus said, My Father worketh hitherto, and I work (John 5:17). I must work the works of Him that sent Me, for the night cometh when no man worketh (John 9: 4). I have finished the work which Thou (Father) gavest Me to do (John 17: 4).

First and foremost, this parable was given to people who are UNSAVED. Is it not natural for people who have little or no understanding of God to prepare ONLY for THIS life? Is it not natural for these same people to believe that proper care and maintenance of their possessions is imperative for a successful and healthy life? If these UNSAVED people are to realize their "foolishness", as Jesus points out, then the SAVED people are going to have to assist in declaring God's intentions for people being stewards of that which is HIS. The problem arises, however, when the SAVED people, TOO, are sometimes just as confused with their blessings! The rich man had no realization as to the value of his soul as he said, "Soul, thou hast much goods laid up for many years; take thine ease, eat, drink, and be merry!" (Luke 12: 19). When God heard what the rich man said about his need for larger barns, God referred to him as being a "fool". Do GOD'S PEOPLE, the SAVED, also have little or no value of people's souls if they fail to address the conditions of loved ones, friends, and family who are lost? Would God think that we were "FOOLS" in His eyes if we are doing the same as the rich man?

#22

STORY FOR THE HEART

DIRECTIONS FOR USING ONE'S SWORD

1. Who says I am lost?

Romans 3:23---For ALL have sinned and come short of the glory of God. (All means everyone needs a Savior)

John 3:18---He that BELIEVETH (trust) on Him (Jesus) is NOT CONDEMNED (lost), but he that believeth not is condemned already (lost), because HE HATH NOT BELIEVED (trusted) in the name of the only begotten Son of God (Jesus).

Acts 4:10,12---Neither is there salvation in any other, for there is NONE OTHER NAME under heaven given among men whereby we MUST BE SAVED (than Jesus Christ) (vs. 10)

2. How come I don't feel lost?

2 Cor. 4:4--- The god of this world (Satan) has BLINDED the minds of them which believe not lest the light of the glorious Gospel of Christ, who is the image of God, should shine through.

1 Cor. 1:18--- For the PREACHING of the cross is to them that perish FOOLISHNESS, but unto us which are saved it is the power of God.

3. How can I be saved?

Matt. 18:11--- For the Son of Man (Jesus) is come to save that which is lost.

John 3:16--- For God so loved that world that He gave his only begotten Son (Jesus) that whosoever believeth in him (Jesus) should not perish (die in hell) but have everlasting life.

Hebrews 11:6--- But without FAITH (believing) it is impossible to please him (God) for he that COMETH (approaches or asketh) to God must BELIEVE that He is (God), and that He is a rewarder of them that diligently seek him.

John 1:12--- But as many as RECEIVED HIM, to them GAVE HE POWER to become the sons of God, even to them that BELIEVE ON HIS NAME (the name of Jesus).

Romans 10:9--- That if thou shalt CONFESS WITH THY MOUTH the Lord Jesus and shalt BELIEVE IN THY HEART that God hath raised Him from the dead, thou shalt be saved.

Eph. 2:8--- For by GRACE (unjustified favor) are ye saved THROUGH FAITH (trust) and that NOT OF YOURSELVES: it is a Gift of God.

4. Can I be saved anytime I choose? No.

John 15:16--- Ye have not chosen me but I have chosen you---

John 6:44--- NO MAN can come to me (Jesus) EXCEPT the FATHER (God through the Holy Spirit) which hath sent me draw (convict or make him aware that he is lost) him.

2 Cor. 6:2--- ..now is the accepted time, behold, now is the day of Salvation. (when God is dealing with you and your heart, That's the time you can be saved)

Romans 13:11--- And that knowing the time, that now it is high time to awake out of sleep, (ignoring God) for now is the salvation (return of God) nearer than when we believed. (first saved)

Matt. 7:7--- Ask, and it shall be given you; seek and ye shall find; knock, and it shall be opened unto you. (if you are sincere, God will save you)

5. How can I live as a Christian (Christ like)?

Gal. 2:20--- I am crucified with Christ: nevertheless I live; yet not I, but Christ liveth in me.

John 15:5--- I am the vine, and ye are the branches; He that abideth in me and I in him, the same bringeth forth much fruit; for WITHOUT ME, YE CAN DO NOTHING.

Luke 10:19--- Behold, I GIVE UNTO YOU POWER to tread on serpents and scorpions, and OVER ALL the power of the ENEMY, and nothing shall by any means hurt you.

1 John 4:4--- Ye are of God little children and have overcome them (the powers of Satan) for greater is He who is in you (Holy Spirit) than he (Satan) who is in the world.

Phil. 4:13--- I can do all things THROUGH CHRIST which strengtheneth me.

6. What do I have to lose if I reject salvation today for hopefully another time?

Heb. 9:27--- And as it is appointed unto men once to die after this the judgment (you don't know when you will die)

John 12:48--- He that REJECTED ME (unsaved), and RECEIVETH NOT MY WORDS (chose to remain lost), hath ONE THAT JUDGETH HIM (God the Father); the WORD (the Bible) that I have spoken the same shall judge him in the last day.

Mark 8:36--- For what shall it PROFIT a man, if he SHALL GAIN the whole WORLD, and LOSE his own SOUL?

7. What do I have to gain? (Besides the ESCAPE FROM HELL)

John 14:3--- I will come again and receive you UNTO MYSELF that where I am there ye may be also. (God's people will be together again)

John 14:2--- In my Father's house are many MANSIONS, if it were not so I would have told you. I go to prepare a place for you. (There are mansions prepared for us there.)

Rev. 21:4--- And God shall WIPE AWAY ALL TEARS from their eyes; and there shall be NO more DEATH, NEITHER SORROW, NOR CRYING, neither shall there be any more pain; for the former things are passed away.

8. How will I know when I'm saved?

Acts 2:4--- And they were all filled with the Holy Ghost. (We too are filled with the Holy Spirit)

Acts 11:12--- And the Spirit bade me go with them, nothing doubting. (The Spirit of God speaks to us through our thoughts)

Romans 8:14--- For as many as are led by the Spirit of God, they are the sons of God. (the Spirit helps us make decisions)

Romans 8:16--- The Spirit (the Holy Spirit) itself beareth witness with our spirit (to us), that we are the children of God. (the Spirit comforts and assures us)

Romans 8:26--- Likewise the Spirit also helpeth our infirmities (life's problems): for we know not what we should pray for as we ought (should pray for): but the Spirit itself maketh intercession (helps us decide) for us with groanings (needed help) which can not be uttered.

9. Will I always be saved?

John 10:27-28--- My sheep (Christians) HEAR MY VOICE and I KNOW THEM, and they FOLLOW ME. And I GIVE unto them ETERNAL LIFE, and THEY shall NEVER PERISH, NEITHER shall ANY man PLUCK THEM OUT OF MY HAND.

Romans 6:23--- For the WAGES OF SIN is DEATH (eternal separation from God and his people in hell) but the GIFT of GOD (salvation) is ETERNAL LIFE through JESUS CHRIST OUR LORD.

1 John 5:13--- These things have I written unto YOU THAT BELIEVE on the NAME OF THE SON OF GOD (Jesus) that YE MAY KNOW (for sure) that ye HAVE ETERNAL LIFE, and that YE MAY BELIEVE on the NAME of the SON OF GOD.

John 5:24--- Verily, Verily I say unto you, he that HEARETH MY WORD and BELIEVETH ON HIM that sent me hath everlasting life, and shall not come into condemnation; but is passed from death unto life.

10. What can I expect in life if I dedicate myself to serving the Lord?

I Cor. 15:19--- If in THIS LIFE only we have hope IN CHRIST, we are of all men MOST MISERABLE. (a Christian's life is not easy)

Luke 21:17--- And YE SHALL BE HATED of all men for my name's sake

Acts 9:16--- For I will shew (show) him how great things he must SUFFER for my name's sake (refers to the apostle Paul) (we may suffer too for Christ's sake)

Matt. 28:20--- Teaching them to observe all things whatsoever I have commanded you: and lo I AM WITH YOU ALWAYS, even until the end of the world.

Jude 1:24--- Now unto him that is able to keep you from falling (being lost), and to PRESENT YOU FAULTLESS (to God) before the presence of His glory WITH EXCEEDING JOY.

Hebrews 13:5--- ..For he hath said I WILL NEVER LEAVE YOU, NOR FORSAKE THEE.

Romans 8:17--- And if children, then heirs, Heirs of God, and joint-heirs with Christ; if so be that we suffer with him that we may also be glorified together

I Cor. 10:13--- There hath no temptation taken you but such as is common to man (there are no new problems), but God is faithful, who will not suffer you to be tempted above that ye are able (God WON'T put more on you than you can handle): but will, WITH THE TEMPTATION, also make a way to ESCAPE (noticeable through faith), that ye may be able to bear it.

#23

STORY FOR THE HEART

DO YOU UNDERSTAND THE PARABLES?

The Bible teaches that Jesus spoke to the multitudes in parables (Matt.13:34). His Disciples were puzzled as to this manner of teaching and asked Him why he did so (Matt. 13:10). Jesus' reply was a two-fold answer.

First, it is given unto you to know the mysteries of the kingdom of heaven (Matt. 10:11). Secondly, to those whose heart was waxed gross (hard), their eyes were closed, and ears dull of hearing, these people would not be able to understand the mysteries of the kingdom of heaven (Matt.13:15).

Did Jesus mean that hidden in the parables were truths for ONLY God's people and how they would be able to live the Christian life? Read the parables and see for yourself. Hopefully they will further open your understanding about God and Christian living rather than be hidden from you as they have been for many others since Jesus walked on this earth teaching them.

#24

STORY FOR THE HEART

THE DANGER OF NOT PRODUCING FRUIT

In the Gospel of John, Jesus refers to Himself as a vine in John 15:1. What purpose is the King of Kings and Lord of Lords trying to make to His disciples when He refers to Himself as a lowly, unseemly, unattractive vine? Would Jesus be trying to show His disciples an example of humility for them to follow? Scripture repeatedly dictates that God's disciples are to humble themselves as little children (Matt. 18:4), that God may lift them up (James 4:10), and that God may exalt them in due time (I Pet. 5:6).

Jesus points out that He is the vine and His Father takes responsibility for His care (John 15:1) as husbandman or caretaker. Jesus follows with reference in John 15:2 that branches that claim to be in Him (Jesus as the vine) but are not, are taken away or pruned by the Husbandman (God the Father).

Does Jesus mean that it is God who watches over His church and prunes or purges? If so, then let us rejoice, when God purges us for more fruit and pray that we may never get pruned out of the vine for failing not to do so!

#25

STORY FOR THE HEART

WHAT WOULD THE FINGER OF GOD WRITE ABOUT US?

Many Americans have the habit of expressing their feelings about someone or something by deforming some public property or structure with slurs or negative expressions. This writing on the proverbial wall for public viewing may not necessarily be intended for universal viewing, but nevertheless our desire to express our true feelings often outweighs any precaution that we inwardly and consciously may consider on the contrary.

I recently preached a message from the Book of Daniel regarding life in Ancient Babylon for God's captive people, Israel. When I reviewed this message, as I would hope each Christian would for each message that he or she hears preached or taught, I realized even more its significance to people everywhere.

The background for the message is established in Daniel, chapter four. King Nebuchadnezzar, who is historically noted as one of the world's greatest kings, had a dream that none of his soothsayers and astrologers could interpret. Daniel, a young Hebrew slave brought to

Babylon during one of Nebuchadnezzar's kingdom expanding adventures, interpreted the king's dream through God's intervention. According to Daniel's interpretation, King Nebuchadnezzar had been given his kingdom by God, Himself, and not of the king's own efforts. Yet, because of the king's defiance toward God in ruling his kingdom, he would be temporarily relieved of his kingdom, lose his mind for a specific time, and be driven out from others to eat grass with the cattle (Dan.4: 32-34). When his mind returned to him, he praised and extolled God Almighty and his kingdom was restored (Dan. 4: 35-37).

Certainly, knowing all that had happened to his father, Belshazzar, Nebuchadnezzar's son, is as much or even more defiant to God when he inherited his father's throne. Belshazzar is given a vision of a man's finger writing on his palace wall, and the message is not favorable. Once again, astrologers and soothsayers cannot interpret the meaning of the vision. The queen, who remembered Nebuchadnezzar's experiences, encouraged Belshazzar to call for Daniel who interpreted the meaning of the vision. The writing of a man's finger on the palace wall was simply, "MENE, MENE, TEKEL, UPHARSIN".

The relevance of this message to each Christian and each Christian church is threefold. First Belshazzar was in trouble with God. So are countless family members and friends of people who even though they may be faithful in attending church today, they do not know God personally. Secondly, although Belshazzar admitted that he had heard of Daniel and his God (Dan. 5: 14), it was not until the queen established greater credibility that helped make the difference in Belshazzar's thinking. Certainly, one would be hard pressed to find people in our country who have not heard about God, heaven, and hell. Yet, as in Belshazzar's situation, maybe the right person has not witnessed to them to help make God more credible. Thirdly, for Belshazzar, the queen's message was too late. For those who have died without God, it is too late for them also.

Many people may often conclude within themselves that it is darkest before dawn physically. These same people may also believe a great recovery experience in their lives is often preceded by a time of great tribulation. God's greatest **Gift to Mankind is in** the **Message of Christians** that Jesus was sent to seek and save that which was lost (Luke 19:10), (John 3:16). This would be accomplished by paying the **DEBT OF DISOBEDIENCE (Roman 6: 23), (Gen. 3: 3) that the Heavenly Father required for a hopeless and lost world! Mankind can either accept the sacrificial death of Jesus Christ on the Cross of Calvary for their sin debt (Romans 6: 23), or they can go to Hell and pay their own debt themselves in person. The debt MUST be paid!**

The interpretation of the writing MENE, MENE, TEKEL, UPHARSIN as delivered unto Belshazzar from the Finger of God meant that Belshazzar had been weighed in the balance (measures) and he had come up short of what he needed to be. His failure to recognize the Holy God that his father had acknowledged meant that Belshazzar's life was soon to be over and someone else would replace him.

How are we being weighed in God's balance? Do we have friends or family members who are provoking God to replace them with someone else who will do what has thus so far failed to have been done? Who is more credible to be listened to than a son, daughter, sister, brother, father, mother, or one's closest friend? What is there to gain or to lose?

According to God's Word, the Gift of God is ETERNAL LIFE in a place called HEAVEN. The wages of sin or disobedience is ETERNAL DEATH. This ETERNAL DEATH is really an ETERNAL LIFE with all of our feelings, emotions, and memory in a place of torments, pain, suffering, eternal black fire in a bottomless pit called HELL (Matt.3: 10-12), (Matt. 8: 12), (2 Pet. 2: 14, 17), (Luke 16: 19-31), (Job 17: 3), (Ps. 88: 6-7), (Rev. 20: 13-15)!

Countless people's lives in the past have been so wonderfully touched with their eternal destinies changed from the humbling acceptance of the Message of the Son of God, King of Kings, Lamb of God, Great Physician, Jesus Christ. He was and still is, the "Man" that books have been written about worldwide.

He was born of a virgin, lived a sinless life, and died on the Cross of Calvary to pay the sin debt for a lost and dying world (Acts 4: 12) (Jn. 3:16). His fulfillment of His Father's REDEMPTIVE plan and glorious RESURRECTION GUARANTEES each Christian an ETERNAL HOME in a place where eye hath not seen, nor ear heard, nor entered into the heart of man, the things that God hath prepared for them that love Him (I Cor. 2: 9).

Sadly, and most tragically is contrasted the also countless millions of people who have rejected the Message of this Man and have or will someday enter a place called Hell. THIS PLACE was prepared specifically BY GOD, HIMSELF, for SATAN and HIS ANGELS for THEIR REBELLION and REJECTION of GOD'S RULE AND AUTHORITY in HEAVEN (Matt. 25: 41), (Matt 18: 19), (2 Pet. 2: 4), (Rev. 20: 10) and **sadly, was not intended for even ONE of His CREATION to go there! Rejection of the Savior of Mankind, Jesus Christ, has therefore, prompted God to enlarge the boundaries of hell (Isa. 5:14)!**

#26

STORY FOR THE HEART

PREPARE FOR A MIRACLE TODAY

Are there really such things that occur, that can be classified as Miracles of God? Most people are familiar with the 10 miracles known as 10 plagues that God performed through Moses before bringing the Israelites out of Egypt. Then, there was also the crossing of the Red Sea and the feeding and clothing of several hundred thousand people for 40 years in the wilderness (Exodus 7-18). Is there a process one can follow as Moses did, to receive miracles?

Joshua was an Israelite who was chosen by God to lead the children of Israel after Moses' death. What had Joshua learned from Moses about God? After Moses' death God spoke to Joshua commanding him to take the people across the swollen, raging, waters of Jordan into the land of Canaan (Joshua 1:2). Joshua listened to the voice of God, believed, and acted upon that belief by faith crossing Jordan as the waters ceased flowing until all the people had crossed over (Joshua 3). Are miracles from God as simple as listening to God, believing what He commands to do, and acting upon that belief?

In the book of Mark, a man who was not a disciple of Jesus was performing miracles in Jesus' name (Luke 9: 49). When brought to Jesus' attention by his Disciples, Jesus remarked that there is no man which shall do a miracle in My name that can lightly speak evil of Me (Mark 9:39). Did Jesus indicate that through Him, His disciples could claim miracles in His name? In John 14:12, Jesus says, "...he that believeth on me, the works that I do, shall he do also; and greater works than these shall he do, because I go unto my Father." Jesus also stated, "I am come that they (His followers) might have life and that they might have it more abundantly" (Jn. 10: 10)!

Does this mean that God wants His children to perform miracles? Yes! What greater miracle is there than to change people's destinies from a place of torments to a place of great joy and peace eternally by simply witnessing to them about the Savior (Acts 4: 12)? What better reason for Jesus to bless us abundantly, than by reading His Word, establish a personal relationship with the Savior, and become a Soul Winner?

In the church where I pastor, a group of women began a successful singing ministry that produced five highly sought after CD's. Although hesitant to broaden their ministry outside the church, their first CD, entitled "Nothing but a Miracle Will Do" became the assurance of God's blessings that they sought. God blessed not only those who attended this little church with their singing, but also launched the group into a highly successful outreach ministry.

Do you need a miracle in your life? Scripture promises God's children can have a peace that passeth all understanding (Phil.4:7), a realistic presence of God in their lives (I John 4:4), and an eternal home where there are no tears, nor death, or sorrow (John 3:16) (Rev. 21:4). All this is freely given by the heavenly Father (Eph.2:8), but not easy to attain. In the way of the receiver, stands one (Satan) who blinds people's minds, so that they will not see the glorious truth about Jesus Christ (2 Cor. 4:3-4).

Satan attempts to devour God's children because of his hatred for God (I Pet. 5:8) and works tirelessly to deceiving the whole world (Rev. 12:9). He knows, however, that his time is short (Rev. 12:12) before he is cast eternally into a lake of fire to be forever tormented. (Rev. 20:10).

Through all of this, however, God's protection for His people is guaranteed (Luke 10:19), (John 10:29), (Isa. 54:17).

Miracles are realistically common throughout God's Word. They are not part of the extraordinary but part of the normal outpouring of God. In the lives of the Disciples, miracles were commonly performed and experienced. Should we be able to experience miracles as Christ's Disciples did? Let us follow the Biblical examples and see for ourselves. Let us listen to the voice of God as He speaks to us through His Word, our thoughts, the preached and taught Word, our prayers, and other avenues that God uses to communicate with us (John 10:4). Let us believe God wants to give what is best for us (Mark 9:23). Let us then act upon this belief with faith by response (James 2:20).

In Malachi 3:10 God says that we are to **prove Him and see** if He will not open the Windows of Heaven and pour out a blessing so great that there shall not be room enough to receive it. If this happened to you, what would you call it?

#27

STORY FOR THE HEART

MAKE READY FOR A CHANGE IN LIFE

The Bible states that all scripture is written by the inspiration of God (2 Tim. 3:16). This means that every verse is God directed and serves a special purpose (Matt. 5:18). God's Word focuses on God, the Father who sent his Son, Jesus Christ to die on the Cross of Calvary for the sins of the entire world (Luke 19:10). This was necessary because of the disobedience of Adam and Eve in the Garden of Eden, and the subsequent curse of sin on humanity (Gen. 3).

The Old Testament centers on God's chosen people, Israel, and their inability to live righteously under God's Commandments. Their acts of disobedience led to their subjection to different tenures of bondage under neighboring powers. At various given times of repentance, God would raise up a prophet to lead them out from under their present hardships (Judges).

The New Testament focuses upon the life of Jesus (Gospels or Good News) and His mission to do His Father's will (John 4:34). The

Father's will was to seek and save mankind from a hell created for the devil and his angels (Matt. 25:41).

God's plan of salvation centers solely upon Jesus Christ (Acts 4:12), (John 14:6), (John 3:16). It was not a plan based upon mankind's works, but mankind's faith in the works of Jesus Christ (Eph. 2:9), (Rom. 6: 23). The Bible teaches that God's will is that **not one person** should ever be sent to hell (2 Pet.3:9). However, rejection of Jesus Christ leaves God no choice. The penalty for sin (disobedience) has not changed (Rom. 6: 23). Jesus, Himself, said that people would not come unto Him that they may have a more abundant life (John 5: 40).

The Bible may be difficult to read and understand. However, the scriptures that lead us to Jesus Christ and how to be saved are clear and easily understood if we are seriously interested. Read the Bible by possibly beginning with the Gospel of John. "Search the Scriptures, for in them ye think ye have eternal life, and they are they which testify of me " (John 5:39).

Be sure of your salvation, for Scripture states that we can know for certain that we have eternal life (I John 5:13). Jesus said that he was coming again unannounced and unexpected. As life existed in the days of Noah, so shall it be also at the returning of the Son of man, Son of God, Judge of the earth, Master of the Sea, King of Kings, Ancient of Days, Alpha and Omega, the Great I Am, The Anointed One and many other names that He deservedly is referred to be identified. When He returns to claim His Church, those who have prepared through acceptance of Christ's finished work on Calvary will spend an Eternity with Him in a place that "Eye hath not seen, nor ear heard, neither entered into the heart of man what God has prepared for them who love Him. (Matt. 24: 37) (1 Cor. 2:9). Make your reservation, **today** (2 Cor. 6: 2)!

#28

STORY FOR THE HEART

HAVE YOU YOUR WEDDING INVITATION?

Our recent celebration of the Easter season not only brought us joy (Luke 1:14) and peace (Phil. 4:7), but inspirational strength in knowing that our Savior is alive making intercession for us before the Father (Rom. 8:26, 34). It was at the first Easter that Jesus instituted the Lord's Supper or Communion to His Disciples "in remembrance of Me" (Luke 22:19). He immediately followed, by detailing exemplary Christian character building, through acts of servitude rather than by exercising authority over others "as the kings of the Gentiles"

(Luke 22:26). Using Himself as an example, Jesus stated that for us to serve others would bring more joy to his Father rather than us being served by others (John 4:34), (Luke 15:7).

As I reflect on my childhood, I recant on many weekends other families would congregate at our home for dinner, socialization, and relaxation before a new workweek began. All the women would work a few hours to prepare a delicious meal. They would first call the men to the table and then the children. When everyone else had been served, the women would eat and clean up the kitchen.

From the above childhood memory, who exemplified Christ's behavior more, the men or the women? Honestly, I can't remember even once of any woman complaining about being served (by themselves) and eating last. I can't help but wonder how many of the men were so concerned about their personal satisfaction that they failed to see true Christian behavior modeled before them?

It is an obvious fact that many churches have been and may still be holding services predominantly through the faith and obedience of its Christian women. God's Word states that these women are a crown to their husbands (Proverbs 12: 4) and assuredly will be recognized at the Wedding Supper of the Lamb (Rev. 19: 9).

#29

STORY FOR THE HEART

ARE YOU LOOKING FOR A DIVERSION?

I have been pastor of Pleasant Will Baptist Church all my life, or so it seems. My memory sometimes seems to lessen the importance of my life before being a pastor and experiencing all the joy God has rewarded me with in this position.

In the church where I pastor, four women who by their commitment to a musical ministry, have helped broaden the outreach of the church as much as anything or anyone. Known as We Sing 4-God, they have released their first CD/tape project after five years together. "Nothing But a Miracle", a collection of twelve easy listening songs of consolation to one's soul, is scheduled for release in May 2002.

I am sure there are times in each of our lives that we long for a miracle when nothing seems to work! In the book of Matthew, the author tells the story of a woman who had suffered with an issue of blood for twelve years (Matt. 9). She believed that if she could just touch the hem of Jesus' garment, then she could be cured! As the crowd around Jesus seemed to create a diversion, she cautiously and carefully approached Jesus and touched him (Matt. 9:20)! Immediately Jesus turned to her and said, "Daughter, be of good comfort; thy faith hast made thee whole" (Matt. 9:22).

How long has it been since we have realized a miracle in our lives? Could it be as simple as a touch from Jesus through faith? The woman immediately received her miracle, not having to wait (Matt. 9:22).

People have many opportunities in church services, revivals, gospel sings, passion plays, and other means to experience the touch of Jesus. It is important to realize that often a crowd hinders an individual's response. However, in this woman's situation, she used the crowd to her advantage. Everything and everyone else became of secondary importance to the woman when compared to her need to get close to the Master.

How badly do we realize our need for Jesus? Jesus said, "Ye will not come unto me that ye may have life" (John 5:40). Could we just prioritize our lives and place our need for the touch of Jesus first, just once? "If thou canst believe, all things are possible" (Mark 9:23). When nothing but a miracle is all that will do in your life, then use the crowd to your advantage, boldly seeking His presence, to touch Him by faith. Remember that if one has a need to be near the Master, He certainly can create the diversion you need.

#30

STORY FOR THE HEART

LOVE WORTH SHARING

As one reviews Jesus' earthly ministry, it might be misconstrued that Christ's desire to do His Father's will often forced Him to overlook or ignore the needs of those closest to Him. Statements in which Jesus asked, "Who is My mother and who are My brethren" (Matt. 12:48) give the impression that Jesus wished to alienate Himself from His family and extend His compassion and care mainly to strangers. Nothing is farther from the truth!

When Christ was on the cross readying to die, one statement He made was specifically directed to His mother (John 19:26-27). Mary was to care for and be cared for by John the Apostle from this time forward. She was to love John as she had loved Jesus Himself, "Woman, behold thy son" (John 19:26). To John, Jesus said, "Behold thy mother!" (John 19:27).

As children grow up, they often openly admit that they love both parents equally, but sometimes add, "I'm really a "Mama's boy"! This statement does not necessarily omit the love of a father but most often reflects a yielding of the adult to the nurture and guidance given through the tender love that only a mother represents.

When my mother died in April of 1984, my life seemed to shatter. I was a "Mama's boy" in every sense of its meaning. I was married and had a wonderful relationship with my mother-in-law. However, a "Mama's boy" needs a mama.

In the years until my mother-in-law passed away, the emptiness that my mother's passing had left me with was filled by my mother-in-law. She treated me in every respect with the love of a mother as she laughed with me joyfully at times and worried about me at others. With her passing, she left a renewed emptiness and sorrow by the void her absence created. I have thought of her often, and God knows the times that she has filled my thoughts with her bountiful energy. This, she shared abundantly even though she was battling cancer. Apostle Paul wrote about people as my mother-in-law when he spoke about love "suffereth long, is kind, envieth not; doth not behave itself unseemly, seeketh not her own (1 Cor. 13:4-5).

The Lord who gave us His great love, (John 3:16) desires us to reflect His love to others (Matt. 7:16, 20) and through others (Eph. 4:6) as my mother-in-law did to me. With men this is impossible, but with God all things are possible (Matt. 19:26). How does God do this? How can one share love so many times without seemingly spreading itself too thin? The answer is simple; love multiplies rather than divides (Jude 1: 2).

#31

STORY FOR THE HEART

WHEN ALL ELSE FAILS, READ THE DIRECTIONS

Many years ago in a country in the Middle East, there lived a people simply referred to as "God's children". These people had been forced against their will to leave their homeland and serve their conquerors. If they were the Almighty God's people, then why did such an occurrence as this happen?

God had expected His children to follow His commandments for living their lives and had declared clearly in His Word that if they would keep His commandments, then they would receive abundant blessings and peace in their lives. If they chose not to keep His commandments, then they could expect His disfavor (Lev. 26). Sometimes we want to blame God's people of long ago for doing so many wrongs. The truth is that they may have simply done too few things right in His sight. Jesus said, "By their fruits, ye shall know My children." (Matt. 7:16, 20).

We have probably all witnessed to people who say they are not saved by their own admission but add that they are not aware of any wrongs they have done to anyone. This may very well have some justification. Again, it is not the wrongs committed that make us lost in God's eyes. The Bible undeniably declares that we are born into sin and the state of being lost. It is the undone deeds that need to be done instead that keep an individual lost! The Bible states that all have sinned and need a Savior (Rom. 3:23). Salvation is a gift from God through faith, because of His unspeakable grace or unmerited favor toward us (Eph. 2:8).

A true understanding of God's Word will reveal a real Heaven to look forward to and a real hell to certainly avoid. There is a real omniscient, omnipotent, and omnipresent God who loves us and wants the best for us. There is also a real created being called Satan whose desire is to destroy God's people and hinder the Lord's ministries because of his hatred for God Almighty (I Pet. 5:8).

Too often people get confused about what's written in the Bible. This may be because of its being misquoted, mistranslated, or simply misunderstood when shared from one generation to another. Americans are probably the most read people in the world. They probably have in their homes more Holy Bibles than any other nation in the world. However, many Americans may be guilty of reading too many books about The Book rather than The Book itself. Americans are bombarded daily to learn more and accept the teachings of other religions rather than the Christian religion our country was founded upon.

Many years ago, God's people found themselves at the hands of a merciless people because they had turned away from the teachings of God and substituted the favors of other people living around them.

They realized too late their foolish decisions. Seventy years later these people received a second chance. What meant the most to them then were not things or relationships with other people. The Bible states that the people then wept bitterly when God's Word was read, and they understood (Neh. 8).

God's people of long ago thought it unimaginable that they would ever **not** have God's favors and blessings. They thought wrongly! If God's people today in the nation that claims "One Nation Under God", think it also unimaginable to not ever have God's favor and blessings and yet make the same mistakes as others in past generations, they too, will have thought wrongly.

Read the Book! Joy in the Lord is your strength (Neh. 8). To avoid reading and understanding the Word of God puts a people in a precarious position of being outside the will and pleasure of a God who our forefathers revered enough to lay the foundation of America for their children and children's children. The Bible states in Judges 2:10 that there arose a generation who knew not the Lord. If this were that generation, where would that leave our sons, daughters, and grandchildren?

#32

STORY FOR THE HEART

MAKING THE MOST OF YOUR LIFE

Many years ago, there lived a man of great faith named Moses. Moses was chosen by God to perform many miracles through God's power and to assume responsibility for bringing God's people, Israel, from Egypt to Mt. Sinai with God's guidance. Moses, however, had not always been a great leader with unchallenged faith.

When Moses was initially called to go and lead God's people to Mt. Sinai, he made excuses and refused to go. God told Moses that He would send his brother Aaron as support, but Moses wanted Aaron to go alone. Even though God became upset with Moses' reluctance, He patiently persuaded him to return to Egypt (Ex.: 3).

It is important that readers realize that it was Moses' decision to **finally** accept to go to Egypt. God did not override Moses' thinking (Exodus 3: 1-4). Moses was simply an instrument that God used to move roughly 2,000,000 people from Egypt to Mt. Sinai, to Canaan, in fulfillment of a promise made by God to Abraham!

There are many people today who have great faith as Moses had and are given tasks and responsibilities possibly as important as those given to Moses. Our young people today have many opportunities to increase their faith and work productively in God's ministries. Assuredly God wants His children to genuinely want to work in appropriate ministries and stop making excuses for avoiding Christian responsibilities until they get older. God also wants His people to be unafraid (2 Tim. 1:7). Lastly, God does not want brothers, sisters, or friends to do, what is someone else's responsibility. These people have their own responsibilities.

God's foremost desire is to work in each person's life in a way that is designed for only that individual. The Bible teaches that allowing God to work His will in our lives is our reasonable obligation for saving us (Rom. 12:1). Because life passes quickly, we need to value the time that we live (Ps. 89:47) for we all must give an account of what we have done for Jesus Christ (2 Cor. 5:10) (Heb. 9:22). It's your life. Make the most of it!

#33

STORY FOR THE HEART

ARE YOU READY FOR THE SOUND OF A TRUMPET?

Sue and I recently visited our daughter and son-in-law at the Courtmore Camp and Conference Center facility near Louisville, Kentucky. This 1550-acre facility is home for hundreds of youths from peak season early May until late September as one of Kentucky's Baptist camping facilities.

While we were there enjoying our grandchildren, along with Bret and LaShelle, I couldn't help but notice that at the time we ate dinner at the Conference Center cafeteria with the campers, there was excellent coordination of approximately twenty or more service personnel handling the responsibilities. I mentioned to LaShelle that I assumed that budgeting must have increased to allow more assistance to the previously understaffed cafeteria workers. Her reply consisted of one word, "Volunteers."

She then elaborated upon the heart of this Baptist camping facility, the support personnel, who gave of their time and energy while seeking nothing in return. "This facility would most likely go under, if it weren't for these workers who came from many different areas for different time periods," she remarked.

The volunteers consisted of young and not so young. There were retirees of whom some came for the summer, while others came for shorter periods of time and came more often. She even spoke of one church where the youths voluntarily came to camp to work during their school spring break! Praise the Lord!

Surely this is indeed what Jesus had encouraged His people to do when He said, the servant is not greater than his lord (John 13:16). Was He asking each of His Disciples to adopt His example of exhibiting the lifestyle of a servant?

It is undeniably true that we live in a busy world. Nevertheless, Christ's commandment to "Follow Me" is a simple one to understand. As My Father has sent me, so send I you into the world (John 17:18). To what purpose have we been sent? Would our purpose in life be to bring glory to the Father as Jesus did (John 17:6)? Would living our lives following the lifestyle that Jesus stood for also help the world believe in the Servant/Savior ministry of Jesus Christ (Matt. 18:11)?

Simply put, Christ taught His Disciples to give of themselves in service to others expecting nothing in return (Luke 6:35). Everything Christ did, He did, so others would follow His example and believe in Him and His Father (John 17:21).

He now sits at the right hand of the Father, interceding on His children's behalf to save them to the uttermost (Hebrews 7:25). It is therefore our reasonable obligation to offer ourselves to the Father as our Lord and Savior Himself did (Romans 12:1). If ever God's people need to be encouraged to follow Christ's example, it is now (John 7:6).

Many people including Christians, work so busily acquiring the abundant life erroneously in hopes of finding happiness (John 10:10). However, Revelations 14:13 clearly states that the only possessions that will follow us after death are our works for God and then Judgment!

Let us work today and each successive day that we may live hoping to be more like Jesus (Romans 8:25) making a difference daily one life at a time. (John 9:4).

If we are reminded that one day we shall all stand before Jesus Christ and give an account of what we have allowed the Holy Spirit to accomplish through us (2 Corinthians 5:10), then a Christian's responsibility becomes more apparent.

With the faith the size of a grain of mustard seed, let the world see us in the fields of harvest that they may believe that we are sent (John 17:21). Let us stand tall and firm in our belief in the Lord Jesus Christ. Then, let us humble ourselves to do the work of a servant as the Master did in obedience to the Heavenly Father (John 17:4). Then and only then, can we receive His unspeakable joy (I Peter 1:8) and have within us a peace that passeth all understanding amid a surrounding world that is unforgiving and life threatening (Philippians 4:7) (John 17:14) (Mark 6:11).

#34

STORY FOR THE HEART

WHEN WE CHECK HIM HERE AND CHECK HIM THERE

In the second chapter of 2 Samuel, the Bible records the transition from the reign of Saul, King of Israel, to that of David. Israel had been left with no king by the deaths of Saul and his son, Jonathan, in wars with the Philistines. This was the final judgment on Saul for his disobedience to the Lord's commandment regarding the Amalekites as given through the prophet Samuel (1 Samuel 15:1-23).

Transition, even with God's approval, is not always accepted as readily as one might expect. Abner, who had been the commander of Israel's forces under Saul, did not wish to relinquish authority and decision-making power so easily. He therefore established Saul's surviving son, Ishbosheth, as the new king of Israel (2Sam.2:9).

At the same time, the tribe of Judah was anointing David as Israel's new king in Hebron with the Lord's blessing (2 Samuel 2:1). David would reign over Judah for seven-and one-half years there in Hebron. This reign over only part of God's people would end with confrontation between the followers of David and those of Ishbosheth. Led by Joab, David's soldiers boldly defeated those of Ishbosheth's under the leadership of Abner. This one incident led to a long war between the house of David and the house of Saul (2 Samuel 3:1).

It seems difficult in retrospect to understand sometimes what provokes God's people to think, speak, and act the way they do. Israel had been promised by God that they would become a great people with their kingdom vast and everlasting (2 Peter 1:11). Oddly, however, what seemed to be foremost on their minds at this time was to find fault and attack one another!

#35

STORY FOR THE HEART

I WISH I COULD HAVE BEEN THERE

I recently visited my daughter and son-in-law who reside in Bagdad, Kentucky, with my two grandchildren. While there, I had the opportunity to discuss their work in church ministry and read a memo they had written to other "Praise Team" members for encouragement. If I may, I wish to yield to the essence of the memo's point made to others. It is as follows:

The 28th & 29th chapters of I Chronicles record King David's farewell address to his kingdom. There were two very important points for which he needed to cast a vision for the future. The first was the building of the temple and the other was the prospect of his son, Solomon, taking over the throne.

If you want to see what can happen when the Spirit of God fills a place in worship and how it can affect the offering, visit the first five verses of chapter 29. David and his people gave over 46,610 tons (93.22 million pounds) of gold, silver, and bronze to build the temple.

I would like to bring your attention specifically to David's prayer and the comments following it:

Read I Chronicles 29:10-20.

On the heels of the outpouring of the Spirit and subsequent spontaneous giving of the large number of resources to build the temple, we find that David turns to the Lord with gratitude and praise. He starts with praising God for His greatness and power, glory, majesty and splendor, His sovereignty over all and His eternalness (vs. 10-11).

Next, David gives credit where credit is due, to God (vs. 12) and thanks Him again (vs. 13). David acknowledges that God is the ruler of all things and the source of all strength and power. What I think is profoundly demonstrated here in David's prayer is the gratitude that almost involuntarily flows from the authentic experience of the presence of the Spirit of God.

What is important to consider is the idea that this was an impulsive reaction to an encounter in a divinely powerful moment. When was the last time that we had a divinely powerful moment? If a recent one doesn't come to mind, chances are it took place, and went unnoticed. If we can recall one, what was our reaction? Was it of instant and immediate gratitude? Were praise and thanksgiving a part of our response?

I know that I often take the blessings of God and the work of God, both in and around me, for granted. This is a dangerous place to be. It is in this place that Satan begins to plant seeds that misdirect us to self dependence.

In verses 14-20, David goes into greater detail with his praise, basically expressing the same things to God but seemingly unable to stop. Read verse 20. What is that last thing David does? He prompts the entire assembly into praise and worship! Think of what it would have been like to be there? David, who wrote much of the book of Psalms and who danced before the Lord (2 Samuel 6:12-21), surely could lead a powerful worship service! Can you?

#36

STORY FOR THE HEART

A PROMISE GIVEN IN GOD'S NAME IS A PROMISE

In Deuteronomy, Chapter 4, Moses is giving his farewell speech to the children of Israel whom he had ministered to and nurtured as a father to his children. As he speaks from his heart, he reminds them of God's plan for their lives. He emphasizes the many promises that God had already fulfilled in the lives of their ancestors and to them as well. He warns them of past rebellions by a few, but their failure as many to resist, had led Israel to a status of discouragement and unfulfilled lives. He emphasizes unreservedly that their faithfulness to God's commandments would lead them unto the land that would be known as home, according to the promises given to Father Abraham.

While certainly speaking with the utmost tone and tenor of a retiring officer, he warns the people of their vulnerabilities of being influenced by the people around them. He focuses most heavily upon the making of graven images learned from the ungodly and says that God is a jealous God who would not condone this. Moses tells them that if they again would take unto them graven images to serve as the heathen, then the Lord would scatter them among their neighbors, and they would be left few.

Because Moses believed that he knew the hearts of the people almost as well as God did, he reminds them that their existence as a nation depended upon calling on God and following His commandments. He repeats the many wonders that God had done in the sight of the ungodly for their benefit and challenged them to name a god that was greater.

The children of Israel had been given the proverbial "world on a swing with a downhill pull" by God to elevate them in the sight of all the world to be recognized as His people if only they would follow His commandments. He proved repeatedly since the days of His obedient servant, Abraham, that He had been and is continually capable of anything that He chooses to do for them. Yet, sorrowfully, because of the power of the god of this world (2 Cor. 4-6), Satan had blinded them. Sadly, Satan has continued blinding masses of people in succeeding generations that followed to this day, leaving them too, hopeless, helpless, weak and without, fearful and futile.

Moses lastly told the Israelites that when they had endured the severity of God's discipline to a point of desperation, then call on God and place themselves into His merciful hands and pray for forgiveness in allowing them to start over again.

Life today is not much different from the times of Abraham when considering dedication and faithfulness to Almighty God and His Church. On the contrary, the percentage of people as population increases, most likely reveals a continually falling away from God with each successive generation.

Advanced technological advancements have drastically altered our physical lives. However, by many people's assessment, these advancements could have created more available time for study and fellowship with God. On the contrary, this time is most often squandered by over scheduling activities of pleasure rather than fulfillment of promises made to our Creator, Sustainer, Comforter, and Judge.

The establishment by God for Israel to be His chosen people was the fulfillment of a Promise made to one man, Abraham. Abraham, alone, believed in one God even though he lived in a city full of nonbelievers. His faith was strong and proven by his obedience to the commandments given him by God. Because of Abraham's faithfulness and obedience, he is recognized and revered today by the people of Israel.

Today, in Hometown, America, if people would choose to, if necessarily, stand alone believing in God and being obedient to His commandments, what would the people of our country think of them; more importantly, what would God think of them? For Abraham's stand, God said, "I will bless you and make your name great. You shall be a blessing. I will bless those who bless you and curse those who curse you. Without a doubt, if God promised this to Abraham, then He will promise it to us; for God is no respecter of persons (Acts 10: 34).

#37

STORY FOR THE HEART

WHICH GATE DO YOU WISH TO ENTER?

In the Book of Psalms, Chapter 105, the psalmist encourages the Israelites to "look backwards" to when He, God, brought the people out of Egypt and into the Land of Canaan. He reminds them of the wonders that He, God, had done to accomplish this. He brought to their attention, lest they forget, how:

1. God had protected His people by suffering no man to do His children wrongly.
2. God had reproved kings for their sakes.
3. God had called for a famine to bring about His will for His children.
4. God had sent a man named Joseph who they put in prison in fetters and iron.
5. This same Joseph, God put in charge next to the Pharaoh to save Israel during a famine.

6. God again had performed many wonders through His servant Moses.

The characteristics of showing gratitude for blessings in their lives varies greatly among those bearing the name of Christian. Some seek God's face as they believe faithfully that their blessed life is the result of God's watch care and blessings for a faithful obedient life. Other people tend to take the easy road to serving the Lord and when their boat overturns, they cry out to God with a renewal of unfulfilled promises. All others fall between the two above.

The psalmist here, is stating that God is simply reminding His people lest they forget (Deut. 8: 11-18) (Deut. 6: 12) how righteous and holy He is, what high ideals that God has for those who love Him, and by far how much Heaven sacrificed to spare a world of sinners. He reminds them that after He made His presence known to Egypt, that when the Israelites left Egypt that the Egyptians lavishly bestowed their gold and silver on the Israelites showing their gladness that the Israelites were leaving Egypt.

Displaying an attitude of ingratitude before someone is at the least a sign of rudeness whether one believes it is deserved or not. Displaying such negative behavior offends and undermines one's credibility as a forgiving and thoughtful Christian following the Lord's example and commandment (Matt. 6: 9-13). Even though one's display of ingratitude toward another person is detrimental to his credibility, one's display of ingratitude toward the Lord is far more serious (Numbers 14: 26: 32).

The Bible states that eternal life through the sacrificial death of the Lord Jesus Christ is the only payment for our sin debt that entitles us to enter the gates of Heaven (John 3: 16). If we, as lukewarm believers, live a partially committed life for the Lord that He rejects, are we showing Him ingratitude for our displeasure toward Him for "providing a plan of redemption that we may avoid a place of torments called Hell? If this is one's thinking, then maybe this individual needs to check the signs (Matt. 24: 30) that he is following. He may be following the wrong crowd of people by entering the wrong gate for eternity (Matt. 7: 13) and is going the wrong way to a place that is certainly to be regretted upon his/her arrival.

#38

STORY FOR THE HEART

SEEK WHILE THE LORD MAY BE FOUND

In the Book of Isaiah, Chapter 55, the reader is thrust into a time roughly 100 years prior to the 70 years of Exile in Babylon. Israel and Judah are existing as a divided nation. Each of these divisions is experiencing periods of prosperity as well as periods of hardship.

It is here noted that although Isaiah bears the name of the book, he is universally remembered as penning only most of the earlier chapters. The additional writers were undoubtedly inspired by God directly since this book is the most often quoted book in the New Testament, over 411 times.

God encourages the people to seek His face by coming to the waters, and he that hath not money, come ye, and buy and eat; yea come, buy wine and milk, without money and without price (Isa. 55: 1) (Jn. 4: 14).

The people are to seek God who offers them eternal life and blessings from His storehouse to care for His people without money. Salvation is free.

The people are hinted at being workaholics and yet not accumulating much (Haggai 1: 3-9). This was due to devoting their lives to fulfilling their own pleasures which was also a reoccurring problem throughout the history of Israel.

God invites them to accept a Covenant between Him and them. They are to seek the Lord while He may be found. This can be accomplished if the wicked forsake his ways and the unrighteous his thoughts. Then as a whole, return unto the Lord and He will have mercy upon them.

This scripture is most repetitive on reminding God's children how loving and forgiving, how faithful and most able, and how patient and tolerable God is, if the people approach Him in the right spirit.

He lastly reminds them that His ways are not their ways; His thoughts are not their thoughts. As the heavens are higher than the earth, so are God's ways higher than the people's. Remember, He tells them, that His Word will not go unnoticed or unfulfilled. It is hinted here that God's Scripture will be there to testify against mankind as a witness at Judgment.

The children of Israel were living in a time when there were times of prosperity and times of hardship *like today*. They were being encouraged to seek God's face by one of the noblest preachers ever, Isaiah. *Like today*, some of the most inspired preachers ever to take the pulpit for God pour out their hearts to entice people to come to the Water that if drunk will quench an eternal thirst. The people are to drink freely and inherit eternal life simply by asking (Jn 4: 14). It seems, however, that the people *like today*, were workaholics and had other plans for their lives than to "make time for church work". Many times, in Isaiah's lifetime, did the people dwell on evil thoughts that were reflected in their wicked acts *like today*. Lastly, God reminded the people to seek the Lord then, because there would be a time that He would not be found. Where or why would this be so?

In the Book of Amos (Chapter 8: 11), God says that He is going to send a famine in the land (world). This will not be a famine of thirst for food. It will be for the hearing of the Word of God. There are very few religious scholars who will not agree that there is at present *"no hunger for the Word of God"*.

When I was just a young child, I remember an occurrence that happened to my uncle's family. They lived along a river in a small town. One day as the two children were outside playing, one of them decided to hide from his brother and everyone else. Choosing the automobile parked in front of their house, the youngster crawled under the car to hide. Being very tired from playing, he soon fell asleep under the automobile.

When his parents failed to find him a while later, they called repeatedly to no avail. A call to 911 brought rescuers who searched the river for a body. The police arrived and began speaking with neighbors about any clues to the child's whereabouts. With both parents nearing hysteria, the youngster awoke from the increased noise of the growing crowd of searchers and crawled out from under the automobile.

The desire for searching diligently for a child that may be in danger can be compared to searching for the Word of God during a famine scheduled ahead in time. The only difference is that here now, when searching for a child, searchers may be fortunate enough to locate the child. During the famine mentioned by Amos, searchers will be wasting their time looking for the Word of God and His accompanying presence as well!

#39

STORY FOR THE HEART

ASK THE RIGHT PERSON AND YE SHALL RECEIVE

In the Book of Luke, Chapter 11, the Lord had just finished teaching the Disciples how to pray. He then tells a story illustrating the compassion of good neighbors and godly people as well, in failing to extend to others what God had repeatedly established by examples for their lives. The story that he told was about a man's friend coming to his house and asking for some food to feed some of his unexpected company. At first the man declined giving of anything. When the neighbor in need began to beg persistently, the man relented and granted the request.

There are times in our lives that our compassion for others is placed on notice. Whether it is to be analyzed by God alone or people around us is not important. The result of our opportunity is so noted in Heaven. It is noted that the substance of any requests is not the issue with God. It is the condition of the receptive heart that matters the most.

Jesus indicates that the substance of what we sometime request from one another is trivial compared to what He had to offer upon our requests. What Jesus has to offer is eternal life through the Cross of Calvary.

When God's people waver on being compassionate to other's needs, the Lord indicates that denial or hesitation is unjustified and so noted. Christ has established Himself as a role model in giving endlessly to those who request. "Ask and it shall be given you; seek, and ye shall find; knock, and it shall be opened unto you. For everyone that asketh receiveth; and he that seeketh findeth; and to him that knocketh, it shall be opened (Matt. 7:7) (Luke 11:9).

#40

STORY FOR THE HEART

WHAT IS YOUR CONCEPT OF ETERNITY?

In the Book of Acts, Chapter 17, the Apostle Paul is on his second missionary journey traveling through southern Asia and into Europe. He is visiting places that he had established churches during his first missionary journey. Seemingly, due to an urgent request from Silas and Timotheus, Paul was rerouted to Athens to wait for the others to meet him there.

Paul, bolstered by the presence and power of the Holy Spirit, preached to the Athenians about their superstitions. Knowing that he was preaching to a people who wanted to be knowledgeable about many things, he shocked them as he preached to them about something they admittedly knew nothing about, the Unknown God. Even though his message fell on many deaf ears, there were enough people attentive to his teaching and believed in Jesus to sow seeds for someone else to water.

Paul told the Athenians that at a time in the past, the Unknown God winked at the people's ignorance regarding such beliefs as they exhibited (Acts 17:30). Most importantly and most controversial, he acknowledged the Lord Jesus' life, death, and resurrection to provide to all people the opportunity to be raised from the dead also. The resurrection of Jesus is often a stumbling block to nonbelievers. It is most likely that this fact is one important reason that "without faith, it is impossible to please God"(Eph. 4: 15).

Even though most of the Athenians did not accept Paul's teaching, they did agree to "hear of this matter again." Most important of all, there were those who "knew no better" who, when told, by faith believed in Paul's teaching.

The words of Jesus in John 6: 44, state that "no man can come to Me, unless the Father which hath sent Me draweth him" (Jn.6: 44). The magnitude of this statement is staggering. The meaning which is written plainly with no hidden precepts states clearly that man does not choose the time that he wishes to be saved!

It is true that all men are given a chance to accept Salvation by the Grace of God (John 3: 16). Thus stated, the correlation to the spoken words of the Athenians is that they may "assuredly hear of this matter again" but that does not mean that the drawing power of God the Father will be present with an invitation of Salvation. Mankind must accept God's invitation when the convicting power of God is present and is indicative of the Father's drawing to Himself.

#41

STORY FOR THE HEART

WHAT KIND OF FRIEND, ARE YOU?

Apostle Paul is given credit for writing more books of the New Testament than any other writer. This substantiates the belief that Paul was chosen of God and had God's approval and guidance in his life and work (2Tim. 1:16 -18).

Paul writes to Timothy who he loved "as his own son" regarding characteristics of a true friend. In reference to one named Onesiphorus, Paul points out that this friend had oft refreshed him (Paul) (2Tim. 1:16). Although Onesiphorus was aware of Paul's often ill-spoken reputation among Jewish believers, Paul states that Onesiphorus was not ashamed of him (Paul) (2Tim. 1:16). Paul adds that when he was in Rome that Onesiphorus searched very diligently to find Paul to listen to his preaching and give assistance, however he could (2Tim. 1:19). Paul ends this short narrative by saying that Onesiphorus had assisted him in many other ways at Ephesus in which Timothy was aware of himself (2Tim. 1:18).

Much can be learned about Onesiphorus in the three short verses allotted him in God's Word. Paul counted him a true friend based upon: (1) *often* Onesiphorus had helped Paul (2) Onesiphorus was *not embarrassed* or *ashamed* of Paul's witness for Jesus Christ (3) Onesiphorus had to extend a *great amount of energy and effort* to be of help to Paul in Rome and (4) Onesiphorus had been *helpful* to Paul *in other places.*

True friendship is not only special but also essential to a relationship's survival. Whether we are younger or older, the lasting peace and joy that comes from knowing the Lord Jesus is often expressed and realized through our friends whose ministries we share.

There are many benefits to being and having friends. Jesus said that we were His friends if we kept His commandments (John 15:14). He followed this statement by saying to His friends, "Ask anything of My Father in My name and it shall be given unto you" (John 16:23). What greater benefits can be realized than this?

Lastly, Jesus stated, "Greater love hath no man than this, that he lay down his life for his friends "(John 15: 13). Jesus literally did this on the Cross of Calvary to provide salvation to all who would come unto Him for forgiveness (John 3:16) (John 1:12), (John 5:24), (Romans 10:9-10). Look them up and read them. He only asks us to lay down our lives willfully for our friends who do not know Jesus as Lord and Savior.

How are you and I valued among our friends? What qualities do you and I possess that people would want us to be their friend? Better yet, what qualities do you and I possess that Jesus would consider calling us His friend? The words of Jesus are as relevant today as when He spoke to His followers 2000 years ago, "Henceforth I call you not servants. . . but I have called you friends" (John 15:15). Fortunately, a friend of Jesus will always have all the friends that he or she will ever need!

#42

STORY FOR THE HEART

KEEP ME IN YOUR WILL SO I WON'T BE IN YOUR WAY

Bible Study

Psalms 25: 1-7

Verse 1 Unto thee, O Lord, do I lift up my soul. *David is the author herein. He acknowledges that not only does he have a soul, but this eternal part of each of us belongs to God and will return to God at death.* Most people today do not acknowledge that they have a soul. They refuse to acknowledge this because it calls for a more in-depth understanding of its purpose.

I had a man tell me that God, Himself, spoke to him. When I asked what God said, he sharply told me that he would not tell me or anyone else. I sat patiently knowing that he was dying to tell me what the God of the universe said to him. In a moment, he fired at me with his finger and shouted, "I told Him that man did not have a soul!" Then I knew what they had discussed.

Verse 2 *O my God, I trust in thee; let me not be ashamed, let not mine enemies triumph over me.* Notice what is foremost on David's mind. David was King of Israel for 40 years. For most of these years David had to fight repeatedly to maintain his kingdom. David acknowledges that his trust for protection is in the Lord's hands. However, he is mindful of his vulnerabilities as (possibly) the position of King of Israel may encourage him wrongfully at times. He adamantly requests of the Lord to never accept or allow him to be ashamed of depending upon God for His guidance and protection.

Verse 3 *Yea, let none that wait on thee be ashamed, let them be ashamed which transgress without cause.* David seems to have some advisers who belittle David's trust in the Lord by following God's lead in "waiting for something that his advisers" disagree. His view of waiting seems to be one of being in the minority.

Verse 4-5 *Shew me thy ways, O Lord; teach me thy paths. Lead me in thy truth and teach me; for thou art the God of my salvation; on thee do I wait all day.* It appears that the heat of his advisers has been turned up for David to act like a king and make his own decisions. If being in the minority, this would be borderline of insubordination of some of his advisors, whether seriously or merely seeking to have more say so in matters. Irregardless, David senses the urgency of taking the matter to God. Show me the TRUTH. I need to know for sure. Teach me as You, God, have done so many times before. I do not and will never doubt that my Salvation is in You, God.

Verse 7 *Remember not the sins of my youth, nor my transgressions according to thy mercy; remember thou me for thy goodness' sake,*

O Lord. *It seems that those around him dragged up some dead bones to provoke guilt feelings that David may not be on such good graces with God as he thinks. These jealous comments may refer to ungrounded accusations to weaken David's faith in the Lord.* It should be noted here that David's thoughts are transferred from worrying about his enemies (verse 1) to remember me, God, for what You, God, have encouraged and made of my life to glean for God's sake. Whatever that David was unsure of earlier has been settled by merely talking to God. If it were that easy to solve David's problems as king, could we solve our much more insignificant problems the same way?

#43

STORY FOR THE HEART

PREPARE TO MEET THY GOD

Isaiah prophesies to Israel (Chapter 8) of a time soon to be when the newly established kingdom of the Assyrians will invade the region of Mesopotamia, which includes Israel, and destroys everything in their path. There is no way to escape for the Israelites. If the people choose to form allegiances with other nations, it will come to nought (vs. 10).

Isaiah openly states that the Lord has told him not to walk in the way that the people walk (vs. 11). They are to sanctify the Lord and fear Him (vs. 13).

Although destruction is inevitable for the Israelites, God promises that He will be a sanctuary to them that seek Him and let Him be their dread (vs. 13). This warning is given to both houses of Israel, Judah inclusive.

During the invasion, many of Israel shall stumble, and fall, and be broken, and snared, and taken (vs. 15). Isaiah is commanded to bind up the testimony that he is given, and seal (undoubtedly to hide for future use again) the law among the trusted of His disciples (vs. 16).

Isaiah affirms his faithfulness to the Lord in that he will wait for the Lord, whose face is hidden from Israel because the "light of the glorious gospel" (knowledge of God) had gone out (vs. 20).

The rebellious Israelites are destined to hunger and fret while blaming their king and God for the dilemma now facing them (vs. 21). As a result of blaming their king and God, Israel will exhibit repeated rebellious behavior in captivity by looking unto the earth for assistance (vs. 22). This will only further their frustrations and increase their troubles as they descend unto the darkness of ignoring the Word of God that would sustain and eventually bring them full circle.

After receiving warnings from the prophets of God about remembering God's commandments, it is understandable why God had written more than once the encouraging reminders of "remember lest ye forget Me" (Deut. 8: 11-18) (Deut. 6: 12) (Prov. 3: 6-16).

George Santayana, a novelist, and poet who was born in Madrid, Spain, in 1863 wrote, "A people who fail to learn from the mistakes made in history are doomed to repeat them themselves!" Armed with this powerful truth for the lives of people today, are we knowledgeable and grounded sufficiently in God's Word, that we will not repeat the mistakes made by the people of Israel in the past.

In Isaiah, Chapter 8, God had instructed Isaiah to warn the children of Israel to prepare for destruction that lay ahead. This would be the result of an often-repeated scenario by their desiring to be as the heathen around them omitting God from their lives. Isaiah pointed out to them that wizards whom the people seek (vs. 19) only peep and mutter. If the Israelites wanted to know guidance for their lives, then they needed to call on their God?

Countless people living today blame anyone, including God, for the failure of grasping, living harmoniously in a restless and unforgiving world. They repeatedly explore various avenues of interest to satisfy an inner search for peace and contentment that continually alludes them in their search for contentment.

In 1980, singer Johnny Lee recorded a popular hit record that the chorus began with "lookin' for love in all the wrong places". The tragic stories of many people's unfulfilled lives result from searching for answers to their problems in all the wrong places.

If we Christians today, as Israel did then, choose to extend the blame for our failures onto someone else, including God, then we too, will leave God no other alternative. The loving, faithful, and omnipotent God who severely disciplined His children then, will no doubt discipline His children accordingly today.

#44

STORY FOR THE HEART

HOW ARE OUR LIVES REFLECTING THE SEASONS OF LIFE?

In the Book of Ecclesiastes Chapter 3, Solomon, successor to his father, David, was bestowed upon by God, Himself, great knowledge and riches for ruling God's kingdom of Israel. Solomon considers life here on the earth and the behavior of people living here. He observes that there are many similarities among the behavior of one generation to another, both in favor as well as detrimental to living a God-fearing productive life. He acknowledges the similarities in verses 1-10 that are common to each generation.

From his observations regarding the habits of humanity, he concludes that man is to rejoice in his labors that God has given him as a gift. Man is to do good in his life being thankful for the gifts that God has assuredly blessed him with. (vs. 11-13).

Why would God do this for man? Solomon points out that God provides bountiful and goodly rewards to His creation so that creation would reverently fear Him (vs. 14). In return, for whatever blessings and favors that God bestows on His people, He requires them to show acknowledgement of gratitude. (vs. 15).

Solomon envisions a time of God's judgment when all people shall give an account of their responses to the different seasons mentioned in verses 1-10. Solomon relishes the thought that hopefully mankind will refrain from his waywardness at some point in time and return obediently to God so that God, Himself, might manifest (vs. 18) Himself to them and bless them accordingly. Solomon ends his contemplations by expressing that man's end is to return to the dust of the ground and all that man has diligently labored to accumulate is vanity (vs. 20-22.

When one's eyes and mind are focused on the fruits of his labor, it probably could be discerned that his eyes are not on God. Therefore, he is walking in a state of little faith at best. When this man dies (Heb. 9: 27), he will leave ALL the fruits of his labor here. Only the labor that had been done for God will remain with the man as he stands in Judgment (2 Cor. 5: 10).

If we living today ignore the consequences of those who have failed in their service to God in the seasons of their lives, how will this knowledge affect our choices made in the seasons of our lives?

#45

STORY FOR THE HEART

THE DESIRE FOR GREATNESS

The commandment by Jesus for us to go unto all the world sharing His Father's message that Jesus died on the Cross of Calvary for the sins of the whole world (John 3:16) (Matthew 28:19-20) is not always clearly understood by all Christians. The Lord Jesus promised power to accomplish this work (Luke 10:19). He also promised there would be people who would need to hear this message, but that those wishing to share it with them would be few (Matthew 9:37).

When the Apostle Paul established the church in Corinth, he overcame a far greater challenge to share the message about Christ than many Christians' challenges living today will ever have to face. He pointed out that God had given to each of His children Spiritual gifts to accomplish His work (I Corinthians 12:4-6). Paul also noted that the Father would give several gifts if He desired, to any one individual to profit the Father's cause (I Corinthians 12:7, 11). All the gifts from the Spirit were to help a lost and dying world understand there was a Hell to avoid and a Heaven to gain by trusting in the finished work of Jesus Christ on the Cross of Calvary (Luke 19:10) (John 3:16) (2 Peter 3:9) (John 19:30).

Yet with all these gifts given to Christians, God instructed Paul (2Timothy 3:16) to point out to the Corinthians that even with the potential success of a Spirit-filled Christian with several spiritual gifts, there was a more excellent way to spread the message of Christ to our families and friends (I Corinthians 12:31).

The thirteenth chapter of I Corinthians details the concept of charity; the greatest of God's gifts, along with faith and hope (I Corinthians 13:13). Charity, as most people perceive it, is a desire to help others, anyone in need. Thus, innumerable charitable organizations have been established. Charity is also understood to be used synonymously for the concept of love.

Most likely, God intended these two concepts to be combined, as an inexhaustible love to give to others in need. An exhibition of this love is that it will lead to a better understanding of God's purpose for us in our lives but also an awareness of God and His plan for others as well. For God so loved that He gave HIS GREATEST LOVE (John 3:16)!

Giving and showing compassion to others was never to be considered a way of attaining salvation, however (Ephesians 2:8) (Isaiah 64:6). Paul wrote this to the Corinthians Christians. It should be noted that charity administered by Christians is noticed and remembered by God (Revelations 2:19) (Revelations 14:13). It also covers a multitude of sins (I Peter 4:8). Emphatically, Paul asserted that a Christian's life was worth nothing without charity (I Corinthians 13:1-3).

If ever there is a time for a more excellent way to be utilized to tell our families and friends about the saving grace of Christ (Ephesians 2:8), it is now (II Corinthians 6:2). If the fields were white and ready for harvest with just a few laborers then, (John 4:35) (Matthew 9:37), what would Christ express about the world we raise our children and grandchildren in today?

Charity is an inexhaustible love within us to share what we have to give to others in need. Isn't that exactly what Jesus accomplished (John 4:34)? Christ's commandment for His children to go and tell is just as relevant to us today as the day it was given then. Christ's disciples struggled to understand and fulfill their commitments to the Lord. It was by no means easy. We sometimes struggle to understand God's working in our own lives and our commitments are sometimes also challenged. A better understanding was given to the Disciples by the Holy Spirit at the time it was needed, and so it will be given to His laborers today at that same appointed time (Mark 13:11).

#46

STORY FOR THE HEART

FELLOWSHIP WITH GOD IN THE GARDEN

In the Book of Genesis Chapter 1, there is a description of God's creation of all that exists. The last and greatest of His creations is forming man from out of the dust of the ground. God is so gracious to the man by placing him in charge over all His creation (1: 26). God then plants a garden that has "every tree that is pleasant to the eye and good for food". God also planted in this garden the "Tree of Knowledge of Good and Evil" and the "Tree of Life" in the midst or middle of the garden. There was also a river that flowed out of the garden to water the garden and then was divided into four other rivers that progressed onward to water different lands (Gen. 2: 7-17).

It is hard for us to visualize what the Garden of Eden looked like. Even in our wildest dreams and imagination, what each tree may have looked like is impossible to describe considering that the Bible states that "eye hath not seen, nor ear heard, neither have entered into the heart of man the things which God has prepared for them that love Him (1 Cor. 2: 9).

What does the terminology, "pleasant to the eye" mean? Does this mean the trunk, leaves, or fruit or something else regarding the trees in the garden? What size of fruit made it pleasant to the eye? If there were many trees that were "pleasant to the eye", how many of these "pleasant to the eye" fruits were eaten to satisfy one's hunger? All of these questions cannot be answered accurately. However, one question may be answerable.

It is not known how long Adam and Eve were in the garden before they partook of the "Tree of Knowledge of Good and Evil" that Adam and Eve was warned to strictly avoid? It should be noted, however, that God had not told Adam and Eve that they could NOT eat of the TREE OF LIFE which located IN THE MIDST OR MIDDLE of the garden also! Being in the middle of the garden, Adam and Eve surely passed by this Tree of Life at different times daily. Since this tree had no restrictions, why did they not partake of its fruit?

The theme of the entire Bible is fellowship with Almighty God the Father, Jesus Christ, the Son, and the Holy Spirit or Comforter. Since God is eternal, He offers as a gift to His created man and woman eternal life also. Would it have been easy for Adam and Eve to inherit eternal life by simply eating from the Tree of Life located in the midst of the garden where both Adam and Eve spent much time? Absolutely (Gen. 3: 22). If only for the sake of curiosity, why did they not even consider this fruit?

Today, the same God who created all that is listed in Genesis and more is still offering eternal life to all mankind free for the asking.

Yet, mankind overwhelmingly has rejected God's offer of Eternal Life for the choice of fruit that is "pleasant to the eye"!

I wonder if the reason that Adam and Eve did not choose to eat of the Tree of Life was simply that it did not appear, without closer examination, to be "good for food" or "pleasant to the eye" (Gen. 2: 9)?

By considering this thought, is the purpose of God's Church to present God's Word as something entertaining and "pleasant to one's eye", or as a guideline to acquire eternal life through Jesus Christ by whatever means? Was the lack of appeal of the Tree of Life to Adam and Eve entirely based upon appearance and/or the realization that Adam and Eve had no thought or concept of "eternal life"?

Would it be safe to conclude that people who reject the teaching of Jesus Christ today, base their decision upon the appearance of the church, both inside and out? Also, it may be true that many people have a difficult time identifying with a concept that is NOT associated with normal living. This is the concept of "living eternally".

The Book of Proverbs describes a man who chooses to do that which is contrary to God. This man is referred to as being a "fool". From the Hebrew, the word "fool" relates to being senseless and determined to make wrongful decisions.

What greater wrongful decision could be made by any people living today than to reject eternal life? If living today in this life is like a vapor (James 4: 14) compared to the next life that is eternal, would someone who rejects this opportunity for eternal life be described as "being determined to make wrongful decisions?

Can we further pinpoint the reasoning of these people who are determined to make wrongful decisions as possibly not knowing fully the choices to choose from? If the choices are found in the Bible, whose fault is it for the people who reject the Bible's authority and directions for their lives?

As people in this life travel from place to place, they must be aware of many different road signs, some especially difficult to follow. Even then, sometimes, people get off at the wrong exits and often must reroute and start over again to properly arrive at their designated destination.

God's children can surely help people with understanding directions regarding their intended destination, whether here or the here after. However, those people who are adamant and insistent on developing a pattern of making wrongful decisions and choices may very well miss their destinations both now and later. Following the incorrect signs to an intended destination can be costly and wasteful. Carelessly following the scenic route of "places and things that are pleasant to the eye" is through the wide gate that is broad and crowded. Unfortunately, this wide gate will not lead one to his/her intended destination as evident upon his/her arrival (Matt. 7: 13)!

#47

STORY FOR THE HEART

AN AFTERNOON WITH GOD ALONG FOR THE RIDE

Recently our church family scheduled a 4-wheeler outing with Mickey and Mildred Chaple, being in charge. Even with three weeks' notice, there were those who frantically worked to accommodate the activity into their schedule. The point made is that people's lives are extremely busy and interfering with one's busy "routine" truly takes an "Act of God".

For those who gathered at Mickey and Mildred's house at 1:00 pm Saturday afternoon, May 24th, one could feel the excitement of an anticipated afternoon of fun with Christian brothers and sisters.

Shortly before 1:30 pm, ten 4-wheelers, each with two abreast headed for the backwoods trails that would be filled with mud holes, creek crossings, steep climbs, and descents, crossing downed timber, and dodging other 4-wheelers in sharp curves and quick stops. Even the pastor would receive his christening on Bottomless Pit #1.

About midway through the ride, lunch was spread at Mickey and Mildred's camp. Grilled hamburgers and hot dogs along with a wide assortment of catered foods from tag along coolers provided a table spread for well over the twenty who made the ride. Blessing on the food given deep in the woods gave one the realization that this group of muddy-faced Christians was quite aware and comfortable with the Lord's presence in their lives.

As the motorcade finally turned homeward, comments of "I Surrender," "Praise the Lord," and "Pass the Pickles" were heard. Upon loading the vehicles and readying to depart, each vowed to go again. It had been a long and tiring afternoon, but surely, the time spent with God's people could not be duplicated at other events or work activities that were past due to be completed.

The Word says that God laughs (Ps 2: 4). Sometimes He laughs at those who foolishly ignore His work, His will, or His intercession into their lives. At other times, surely, He laughs when we behave as some may think as little children. It needs to be noted however, that Mark 10:14 states the words of Christ. . . Suffer the little children to come unto Me . . . anyway they wish. . . riding a 4-wheeler included.

#48

STORY FOR THE HEART

AN OPEN MIND ON AN OPEN HIGHWAY

In Matthew 28:19-20, the Scripture says from Christ's own words that we are to go, teach, and baptize in the name of the Father, Son, and the Holy Spirit (Matt. 28: 19-20). These words seemed to have more meaning to me as my family was cruising along Interstate Route 81 toward Harrisburg, Pennsylvania, on our way to our daughter's house in New York.

Living my entire life in rural West Virginia, I must admit my apprehensions for visiting the "Big Apple" where my daughter and son-in-law worked. Yet, the farming areas that we traveled through and the innumerable orange and white barrels dotting the interstate began to remind me much of home. Therefore, I would promise myself to be open-minded to opportunities for witnessing to whomever God would open a door to me.

Upon declaring my pledge, God immediately brought to my attention, an elderly gentleman and three distinguish looking companions at a rest stop in Maryland some miles back. The gentleman had been taking pictures of his companions among the spring flowers in front of the backdrop of a natural reservoir high in the Appalachia Plateau. I thought that I would volunteer to take a picture of all four people and offer one of the PRAY coins that I had brought from the church. However, as I hesitated too long, they slowly began walking along the grassy area searching for some shaded sheltered seating, and the opportunity eluded me. I silently prayed NOT to miss my next opportunity.

As we traveled onward, school buses crossed the overpasses, homes were easily visible scattered throughout the countryside, and the bursting blooms of the northeastern fruit trees seemed to be so much like life at home.

Entrance into New Jersey was quite a contrast to the previous two hours of driving. Interstate 78 widened to three remarkably smooth lanes carrying us comfortably through an almost litter free rustic countryside setting. We were now only an hour or so from our destination and already the long drive seemed to fade into the conversation of our new viewpoint of life in New England.

Upon arriving at Leigh and Tadd's apartment and getting settled in, time became more precious as plans were beginning to be made to "see it all". I slipped out and took a walk around the housing complex. There I met Fernando, a Latin American grounds keeper for the complex. He quite cordially received the PRAY coin with my witness. I took his picture, and he took mine. Later that evening, I met Sheral, a mother of two small girls who thanked me with a smile as I gave her a PRAY coin and my witness.

PEOPLE LIKE YOU

I began to sense that maybe my fears that New Yorkers would be uninterested in my witness for Jesus Christ was the result of my prejudice. On my next walk, some distance ahead of me, a heavy-set black woman began her morning walk with her dog. As I caught up to her just as she was turning onto another street, I spoke and offered my testimony and a PRAY coin. She smiled, received the coin, and returned her own testimony for Jesus Christ. I passed on and as I completed my next circuit around the complex, I noticed her standing on the street below, stopping and reading the wording on the coin. In all, I shared my testimony for Christ with nine people, of whom eight graciously received the PRAY coins or bent nails in the shape of a heart. Only one refused my request for only 30 seconds of her time, but she was very polite.

I thought about the image that is personified of New Yorkers by many outsiders, and I thought also how my views of them had changed. At first, I thought as we drove through the streets of New York, that they were the WORST drivers that I had seen. After a while, I concluded that they are possibly the BEST drivers!

As we progressed through downtown, I first thought that these people were the RUDEST people that I would meet. After walking along the streets, I concluded that they were the most PATIENT people that I had met for a while. Last of all, I initially thought that most New Yorkers were probably LOST WITHOUT CHRIST! I had to admit that of the first nine people who I witnessed to, eight received my testimony quite cordially. I now have renewed my thinking. I admit that my prejudices and fears toward New Yorkers were unfounded and unjustified.

Prejudice, even in seemingly insignificant situations, can lead one to the practice of more harmful prejudices. As innocent as simple prejudice may appear, its thinking is in quite contrast to what Jesus Christ stated clearly as to how his children are to think and speak (Matt. 7: 1-3). Many times, the Lord utilized His valuable time to listen and respond to the needs of those who were classified as outcasts by most of the people. Many of these outcasts, after leaving the presence of the Master, however, became avid worshippers of God. Their new lives for God would be recognized with little fanfare here among the people who knew them so well. In Heaven, however, "there would be far more rejoicing over any one sinner who repented and therefore was so noted in God's records" (Luke 15: 7) (Rev. 13: 8) (Rev. 21: 27).

#49

STORY FOR THE HEART

LET'S TAKE OUR STAND WITH SWORD IN HAND

Too often today, God's people erroneously believe that problems they encounter in the 21st century are unique when compared to those experienced by Christians in the Scriptures. Although the process of human behavior has changed greatly in HOW problems are experienced, the degree of human disappointment that is associated with these problems, however, has changed little.

As American service men and women are involved in warfare far from home, so the children of God, found themselves far from their homeland unable to return, prisoners for some 70 years (Nehemiah, Ezra). One such captive, Nehemiah, became quite concerned about the remnant of unskilled and aged people left in Jerusalem at the time of the captivity. Nehemiah expressed his concern to the king in Shushan where although he was a captive, yet God had given him favor as the king's cupbearer (Neh. 1: 11).

The degradation of Jerusalem had reduced life there to a mere survival. Nehemiah shared this with the king tearfully (Neh. 1: 4).

Just as true today, these circumstantial situations of broken hearts and lives, have in each generation been Satan's greatest means to discourage God's people. Satan's intent is to slow God's work in churches throughout this great country. Yet repeatedly, God's Word assures us of His protective care (Luke 10: 19; 1 Pet.5: 7) and prosperity (Mal. 3: 10; John 10: 10).

When Nehemiah prayed to God for assistance (Neh. 1:5), he FIRST acknowledged the Father with RESPECT before he gave his REQUEST (Neh. 1: 6-11). God's people today, often pray in a hurry, resulting from a hurried lifestyle to the brink of desperation, overextending time and tolerance levels.

His unusual request to the king was to be allowed to return to his homeland to check on those living there. Strangely enough, Nehemiah was given permission to do so.

As Nehemiah inspected the ruins in Jerusalem upon his arrival, he encouraged his brethren through his FAITH, ENTHUSIASM, and WORK ETHIC. The people responded (Neh. 2: 17-18). In Nehemiah 3: 1-32, the Scriptures are filled with the workers standing side by side working together as a united effort of all toward a single purpose.

Would it be too much to ask those who attend our churches today how many are willing to stand next to one another and uniformly share the work of the church when there is work, both physical and spiritual, to be done? Too often, too few people carry too heavy a burden in dealing with the responsibilities of church work!

After Israel's jealous neighbors caused several work stoppages, the building of the wall around Jerusalem was completed. Nehemiah had refocused the people's attention from WHAT HAD BEEN to WHAT COULD BE, from OBJECTS and MATERIALS to LIVES WEIGHING IN THE BALANCE and gave them an inner assurance of SUCCESS WITH GOD WAS CERTAIN. This premise has not changed for each generation from an unchanging God (Mal.3: 6).

Church ministries that are successful today are those like Nehemiah that follow God's leadership in a united effort for a cause worth dying for. Our motivation and strength to work comes NOT from the one BESIDE us, but from the One who is WITHIN us (1 John 4: 4). Ten times did the enemy challenge the workers on the wall with words of discouragement (Neh. 4: 12). Yet the task was completed.

How many times does it take the enemy, Satan, to share discouraging words with us today before we say as the workers then had PREVIOUSLY STATED, "the strength of the bearers of burdens is decayed, and there is much. . . so that we are not able. . (Neh.4: 10)? God's Word should resound repeatedly His patience and mercy; I am the Lord, I change not; therefore ye. . . are not consumed (Mal. 3: 6).

Most assuredly, it is OUR TIME to seek God's mercy and forgiveness with a broken heart and contrite spirit (Neh.1: 4-9) Psa.51: 17). It is OUR TIME to stand side by side with one another doing God's work for the sake of lives weighing in the balance (Neh.4: 14). It is OUR TIME to accomplish the church's work as Nehemiah pointed out, with ONE HAND on the tool we are working with and on guard with the OTHER HAND holding our Sword (Neh.4: 17)!

#50

STORY FOR THE HEART

DEATH AS A GATEWAY TO PASS THROUGH

When God called me to preach some years back, I was terrified being in His presence. After He lessened the power of His awesome presence, I overcame my fear relinquishing my will and embarked upon the most exciting time of my life.

Since being in the ministry, I have also had the opportunity to have been a part of several funerals and weddings, and sincerely must say that some of my most rewarding times in the ministry have been on these occasions. Recently, I preached the funerals for two special friends of my family. I spoke about death and its purpose for being administered upon humanity.

In the Book of Genesis, we see that Adam and Eve were told by God that if they ate of the tree that was in the center of the garden, then they would surely die (Gen. 2:16-17). Because this forbidden fruit was eaten, Adam and Eve died along with humanity. Initially, this seems like an unjust punishment for all humanity for the disobedience of just two individuals! We have a different perspective, however, when we look at the Scriptures. In Romans 3:23, Romans 6:23, and Isaiah 64:6, God's Word teaches us that ALL humanity has in turn, as Adam did, become disobedient, that the price for such has NOT CHANGED, and that our ability to live a righteous life pleasing to God is IMPOSSIBLE!

Although death was administered by God as a discipline, Satan has utilized it as his greatest weapon to cast fear and sadness upon God's children. Scripture is clear to note that the death of a child of God, a Christian, is to be a joyous occasion (John 14:28). It is an appointment for ALL and a GATEWAY back to God (2Cor.5:8), (Heb.9:27), (Luke 23:43). God's Word states that when a Christian dies, he is blessed, for he now rests from his labors (Rev.14:13).

Until death receives its final reward at being cast into the Lake of Fire (Rev.20:13), humanity will be required to die both physically and spiritually. The spiritual death of an individual without Christ, is clearly defined as an eternal separation from God, being cast into the Lake of Fire, and an experience in everlasting torments (Rev. 20:6), (John 3:16), (John 11:25-26), and (1 John 5:13). This death is AVOIDABLE through JESUS CHRIST (Eph.2:8), (John 3:16).

Human nature often causes one to shudder at the thought of death. Even God's children become burdened with a troubled heart (John 14:1-5) at death's seemingly permanence. If one were to view the full impact and result of death, then perhaps it might be more easily dealt with in families today. It was in the beginning and remains today, to those who believe in the Scriptures, a discipline, and a gateway back to God (1Pet. 4:19, Ezek. 18:4).

When time ceases to be as we know, the Trump of God will sound, and Christ shall step out onto the clouds to receive His children; then there will be no more death, nor sorrow, nor crying, nor pain for the former things will have passed away and mankind will be free at last (Rev. 21:4), (1Thess.4:13-18).

#51

STORY FOR THE HEART

HOW STORM WORTHY IS YOUR LIFE?

Recently I preached a series of sermons on storms that come in our lives. I sincerely believe that these sermons have had more a profound effect on my ministry than any other sermon or series of sermons that I've preached. For those who may not have been present at Pleasant Will Church, may I share the essence of these messages?

First let's establish some truths about storms, whether physical or spiritual:

1. Storms will come into our lives. (Ps. 23)
2. Although they seem to last forever, they have a beginning and an end to them. (2 Cor. 4: 17-18)
3. God knows our thoughts, where we are always, and is walking through these storms with us. (Isa. 43: 2)

4. Although we may seem the <u>lesser</u> because of the damage incurred from the storm, survival in the storm grants us a <u>greater</u> value.
5. A vessel's worth is not based upon its appearance or its claims of value, but on its reliability to carry its cargo to its destination. (Mark 14: 3-9)

From the first message relating to the storms in the church at Jerusalem (Acts 8:1-40), we find that Philip was in God's will, in God's church, and experienced great persecution for his faith (Acts 8:13). God's children thus learn that often the greatest storms or attacks delivered toward them from Satan are directly related to their firm commitment to Jesus Christ. Thus, we also are to expect the storms and examine their purpose for our lives.

The second message taken from Acts 17:10-32, shared seven reasons why a church may experience storms. These include:

1. Failure to stand for its beliefs.
2. Failure to see its field for ministry.
3. Failure to witness for Jesus Christ.
4. Failure to change from traditions and superstitions.
5. Failure to realize its source of power.
6. Desire to remain ignorant.
7. Desire to procrastinate its responsibilities.

The third message related to Jesus being tempted in the Wilderness (Matthew 4:1-11). He first fasted for 40 days, which seemed to be a weakening experience rather than a strengthening one. We may be able to learn from this experience that by weakening the physical man, this gave an added edge to His spiritual being within Him. This is substantiated by the temptations offered by Satan. The temptations appeared to be directed toward the physical side of Jesus to counteract His spiritual being.

The last of the four messages was taken from Luke 4:14-30. Jesus had just defeated Satan in the wilderness and immediately thereafter began His ministry. The importance of this act is that after the wilderness experience, Jesus chose a good offense as a defense to continue to defeat Satan. Apostle Paul wrote in Romans 7:19, "For the good that I would, I do not; but the evil that which I would not, that I do." Therefore, the point derived from this message is that once a storm has passed (as in Jesus' wilderness experience), we are to move quickly into our ministries, or we may find ourselves drawn back into the storm to relive and experience its impact again and again.

Paul wrote that if in this life only we have hope in Christ, we are of all men (and women) most miserable (I Corinthians 15:19). The point made is that Christians are to put on the whole armor of God (Ephesians 6:11), pick up their Sword (Ephesians 6:19) and live their lives by following Jesus one storm at a time, remembering once again, "A vessel's worth is not found in its appearance or its claims, but rather in its reliability to carry its cargo to its destination!"

#52

STORY FOR THE HEART

SPOKEN TO BY THE GREAT I AM

William and Bethel were married and lived in the same little town for most of their married lives. They had several friends and enjoyed the quiet life that a small rural town provides. The longer they lived in this community closer friendships were developed for each of them with other people. As they grew older together, it was William whose health began to fail first. After repeatedly being treated for various illnesses, William was diagnosed with cancer.

William's personality changed as he became more difficult to treat and reacted often negatively to Bethel's attempts to care for him. The longer that Bill lived with the cancer, the more difficult it was for Bethel to take care of him.

Their relationship suffered greatly and Bethel's health too, began to suffer. When William's cancer continued to progress, a close friend of theirs called me and asked me to go visit with them and talk to them about God. I was pleased to go and was welcomed graciously inside their home. We talked of several different subjects until God gave me a window to introduce the Lord Jesus Christ to them. William listened to me, but repeatedly rejected any requests of mine to accept Christ as his Savior. Bethel showed much less interest in my conversations about Jesus Christ.

The worse that William's cancer developed, the less William seemingly was interested in the subject of God. It was not until I spoke about the mercy and unmerited grace of God that William listened. He broke down when I told him about God who had created and prepared a place that "eye hath not seen, nor ear heard, nor entered into the heart of man, what God had prepared for them that love Him (1Cor. 2:9). It was then that the convicting power of the Holy Spirit worked favorably in William's life, and he accepted Christ into his life.

The family asked me to speak at William's funeral although I was not a preacher at that time. I spoke of the times that I visited William and how he had been saved. I ended my talk by saying, "the last time that I saw William, he was on his way home."

It was almost two years after William had passed that Bethel became ill and was taken to a nursing home in Glasgow, near Charleston. The same individual who had asked me to visit William asked me to go talk to Bethel.

Not having too many friends who could travel to Glasgow, Bethel was glad to see me and welcomed me wholeheartedly. After being there for almost an hour, I mentioned God. She seemed so careful not to hurt my feelings, but she said that God may have been what William needed, but not for her. Her continued conversation seemed to indicate that because of their differences and William's mistreating of Bethel, if William were going to Heaven, then she didn't want to go!

At the time I thought of how childish her answer was. However, I visited Bethel several times there in the nursing home and each time she firmly rejected me discussing the church, God, or my experiences as the adult Sunday school teacher at Fairfield.

Bethel had been in her seventies when I first became acquainted with her and William. It had been almost two years since William's passing. Bethel's mind was reasonably clear, but she was beginning to forget more things that we had discussed each time that I returned. I continued to visit and with each visit, I would always attempt to talk to her about God. It seemed that she enjoyed me mentioning God so that she could smile and reject my witness.

One day, out of frustration for her rejecting my attempts to discuss God, I asked her that since she had rejected my testimony about God, would she listen to God, Himself, if He spoke to her. With a pause and a shocked look on her face, she spoke plainly, "Yes, I would." I prayed and left.

There were many activities going on in my family with two growing teenagers at this time and I just simply forgot about Bethel for about a month. One evening, God clearly placed her on my mind. The first available day that I had an opportunity to go see her, I did.

As I entered her room, she was talking to a nurse beside of her bed. When she noticed my entering the room, she smiled broadly and said, "Well, here's my pastor!"

Immediately I knew something was different. She had never referred to me as her pastor. As the nurse left, I stepped up beside her bed. Her face lit up like a Christmas tree and she said, "Mike, He spoke to me."

I smiled back and said, "What did He say?"

With tears pouring from her eyes, she said that He told her to get down on her knees! She then said that although she had not been out of bed for over two years, she called two nurses to get her out of bed and help her to her knees. With eyes bright and glistening from tears, she said, "Mike, He saved me."

The next time that I returned to see her, I brought her a cactus that had bloomed. I told her that this cactus was her life. As the cactus, being an older plant had bloomed late, so had she. She was so happy, and I was so happy for her. It was about three weeks before I got to return to the nursing home. When I found her room empty, I asked where she was. The head nurse's answer was clear. She has passed on.

This answer was true. Bethel had passed on to better and higher things. Her bitterness and burdens that she had once carried were gone. She was headed home. The time of her giving a testimony for the Lord was relatively short, but the tears in her eye and the glow on her face would surely be remembered by those who had met and known her before and after the Great I AM had spoken to her!

#53

STORY FOR THE HEART

ARE YOU LISTENING FOR THE TRUMPET?

Does anyone care about me or want to hear what I have to say ANYMORE? These are words of frustration most of us have issued at some time in our lives when discouragement seemed to overwhelm us. We then may feel that our lives have been transferred from a place of satisfaction and acceptability to one overshadowed with rejection. Family crises, personal health problems, financial disasters, and countless other dilemmas face many of God's children defiantly each morning they awake. As the steady dropping of a raindrop can wear away the concrete below, so Satan works to frustrate, weaken, and discourage Christians to channel their focus of faith in God to finding their own way through a world of darkness without THE LIGHT of the WORLD. (Jn 9:5).

The Bible teaches that before Christ returns, there will be a falling away of people from seeking God (2 Thess. 2:3). No one is exempt from Satan's attacks to fulfill this prophecy. Apostle Paul, one of the greatest Christian role models in the New Testament, wrote that he was a wretched man experiencing warfare within himself. There were times that he did "that which he didn't want to do while at other times not doing that which he wanted to do" (Rom. 7:14-25).

In each of our lives we experience victories and defeats. We learn to repent and rebound, however, each time. Hopefully, as David did as recorded in I Chronicles 21:13, we too, should place ourselves at the mercy of the Lord knowing that Satan knows our vulnerabilities and uses them repeatedly against us (Heb. 12:1).

Let us, as Christians, firmly BELIEVE the truths of God by reading His Word daily and prayerfully seek His will for our lives. Let us LEARN from our mistakes and failures and DISCARD from our minds the thought that God has abandoned us. Let us REMEMBER the times in our past when our survival depended solely upon His hand leading us through the "valley of the shadow of death" (Ps. 23).

For those people who do not know Jesus Christ in forgiveness of their sins and have passed on, it is too late to get their house in order (2 Kings 20: 1). Life, as people are accustomed to living, is about to change dramatically. Time as we know it, will cease to exist as God removes His children from planet Earth with great grandeur (1Thess. 4: 13-18)! Those remaining will be left trembling and calling for the rocks and mountains to fall upon them to hide them from the FACE of the ONE who sitteth upon a Great White Throne and the wrath of the Lamb (Rev. 6: 15-17), (Rev. 20: 11-15), (Rev. 22: 12-14)!

#54

STORY FOR THE HEART

THE PASSION OF CHRIST PASSED TO OTHERS

Our church, Pleasant Will Baptist Church, has just completed a series of revival meetings with four different evangelists. The meetings were well-attended especially by members of neighboring churches. Inspirational singing supported God-directed messages provided a true revival spirit.

The messages were related specifically to Christians losing their zeal for God's work. Although the Christian is guaranteed eternal life in Jesus Christ, each Christian has family and friends who, without Christ, do not have this guarantee and are bound for eternal torments in Hell (Luke 16:23).

It is also noteworthy to mention that the Sunday morning prior to the revival Deacon Basset Wallace Smith preached his first message after being called into the ministry. His Scripture text, Luke 16:19-31, was the identical Scripture, Evangelist Mike Davis used on the last night of scheduled meetings. Thus, our revival meetings began and ended focusing on the lost.

I am old enough to remember the "old-time" revival meetings experienced as a child. The revival meetings were not in competition with other social functions then as they often are today. They WERE the social function! There was a spirit led and blessed service that even a child could sense, experience, and be in awe of its effect upon those present.

The Bible states in Judges 2:10, that there arose a generation who knew not the Lord. How could this happen? Whose fault could this be? With uncertainty, we must wonder whether our children will have as vivid memories of pleasant childhood experiences attending church activities as some of us.

At the recent revival services there were several children who attended so the church reserved the first three pews for youths on the final night of services. Participation such as this, as well as scheduled monthly youth involvement activities, is planned to encourage youth self-esteem and self-awareness to foster Christian growth. Realistically we must all acknowledge that if children's faith is at best, as strong as their parents' faith, will this suffice for the next generation's children?

Jesus Himself said, "When the Son of Man cometh, shall He find faith on the earth?" (Luke 18:8). This statement seems to indicate the possibility of disintegrating faith of God's people from one generation to another. Does this propose the possibility there will be a repeat of Judges 2:10 in our lifetime?

God states in his Word, "Remember now thy Creator in the days of thy youth, while the evil days come not, nor the years draw nigh, when thou (youths) shall say, I have no pleasure in them" (I don't want to go to church) Eccl. 12:1.

The wisest of all men, Solomon, finished this chapter by saying, "Let us hear the conclusion of the whole matter: Fear God, and keep His commandments; for this is the whole duty of man" Eccl. 12:13.

Revival services have been held for countless years. Several objectives are sought by these services including salvation of the unsaved and the rekindling of God's will in the lives of people who claim Christ as their Savior.

The Apostle Paul wrote, however, that to live Christ-like as the name Christian implies can only be realized by Christ living His life in His children. (Gal. 2:20). If Paul believed this about his life for Christ, then should we believe it for our lives also?

#55

STORY FOR THE HEART

DO YOU WISH YOU COULD HAVE BEEN THERE?

To establish the foundation of the early Christian Church, the Lord God depended heavily upon the faith and fervor of a few dedicated Christians who the Lord called personally. Initially, they showed great enthusiasm in finding the "Messiah" and sharing this Good News with others (John 1: 41, 45). They spent three years traveling throughout Israel listening and learning from the teaching of this Master. They watched intently as He dealt with each situation with great interest and concern.

The people that the Lord preached had many questions regarding His teaching, and faithfully followed Him from one place to another. Being drawn to Christ by His godly attributes to deliver manna to a people who hungered (1Cor. 10:3), (John 6: 31-63), (Rev. 2: 17), the multitudes returned again and again to listen intently to His messages. They recognized His power over the forces of evil that seemed to be so rampant throughout the land touching so many of their lives (John 5: 1-18).

His Disciples, at times seemed to downplay the very acts of the miracles that Christ performed, while focusing more on the worthiness of those seeking Jesus as to whether they were wasting His time or not (Matt. 15: 23) (Luke 9: 12). He repeatedly cautioned His Disciples about the power of the Holy Spirit within them and impressed upon them the usage of this power in an unacceptable manner (Luke 9: 54). They were to learn the ways of Jesus to be able to follow His example in furthering His work in establishing His Church when the time of His departure became imminent.

Christ, upon their request, taught the Disciples how to pray (Luke 11: 1). He not only prayed for them, but also prayed for **those who would believe on the Disciples' preaching and writings** (John 17: 9) (John 17: 20-26). Is it not discernable that Jesus, therefore, prayed for Christians today who believe on these same Disciples' writings? The names of **All** of God's Children are written in the **Lamb's Book of Life** (Rev. 13: 8). Before leaving Earth, humanity may want to check the Book to see if his/her name is written therein (Romans 10: 9-10) (Jn. 3: 16) (Acts 4: 10-12) (2 Tim. 3: 16)!

Apostle Paul was also a hunted man, along with the Disciples for the cause of the Gospel. Paul suffered physically several different times and even was left for dead after being beaten and stoned by envious Jews (Acts 14: 19). Paul's command and control of his ministry for the Lord was accompanied by the Lord's power and presence providing protection and proof that the Word of God will accomplish what it is intended for and will not return void and unfulfilled to God (Acts 28: 3).

The success of not only Paul's ministry, but the Disciples' ministries as well was evaluated by the Jews at Thessalonica on Paul's second missionary journey. When the disgruntled Jews searched for Paul as a large uncontrolled mob and could not find him, they asked unto the rulers of the people there, the location where Paul and any others who were preaching with him might be found. Their accusations centered upon Paul and any others whose message that they preached "was turning the world upside down."(Acts 17 6)

How is it possible that so few witnesses could accomplish so much and make such an impression on so many? The Scriptures are clear in that "all things are possible with God" (Matthew 19:26) (Mark 9:23), (Mark 10:27), (Mark 14:36), (Luke 18:27). Did these first few Disciples have extraordinary powers that made them different from Christians today? Were they given unseen assistance for support by the Lord that may be deprived from many Christians living today? (2 Kings 6: 8-23)

These first few disciples were looked upon by others as unlearned and ignorant (Acts 4:13). They often struggled to grasped Christ's teaching (John 14:22), (Luke 9:45), (Luke 18:15), (Luke 22:24), (Luke 24:11). They failed Christ (John 18:17-27), (Mark 16:11) (Matthew 17:19-20). However, they forsook all, (Matthew 20:27) and although they struggled while He was with them, after Christ had been crucified and risen, they began the greatest ministries ever, depending upon the Holy Spirit (Comforter) whom Jesus promised to supply their needs (John 14:26), (John 15:26), (John 16:13-14), (John 16:7) (Mark 13:11).

Since God is no respecter of persons (Acts 10:34) the success of these early Disciples was based solely upon their determination to please the Master EMPOWERED by the Holy Spirit. Even with their failures, they allowed God to have more and more control of their lives as He changed and softened their hearts to GIVE what they were given rather than to KEEP what they might need for later use! Christ had told them that He took care of the flowers and birds (Luke 12:6-7) (Matthew 10:29-31) (Matthew 6:28-31) and that He would take care of them (and us) for they (and we) were worth more than MANY BIRDS (Luke 12:7) (Matthew 10:31).

Let us remember that serving the Lord is a choice. Many of God's people throughout the generations have pledged their loyalty to Christ, only to weaken this loyalty by lessening the time and use of their talents, for the advancement of the kingdom of God. Their commitment lacked complete dedication. Their choices of selecting the approach of less resistance resulted in empty and unacceptable choices to "whether is it easier to do" (Matthew 9: 5), (Mark 2:9), (Luke 5:23).

Is it easier to READ the Word and respond, or claim aloud an inability to be unable to understand the language? Is it easier to ATTEND church services that satisfy the hungering for the Word of God or STAY AT HOME and enjoy the pleasures of sin (disobedience) for a season? Hiding one's gifts of time, talent, and treasure that God has granted each of us for the use of sharing His Word will only bring sorrow in this lifetime, but far greater sorrow in the next.

The same Holy Spirit that motivated the early Disciples lives within us Christians today (1 John 4:4). God, Himself, is in most homes in America because God's Word IS God (John 1:1)!

If we had a difficult time understanding the Word, so did the early Disciples. If we fail Him, so did the early Disciples. If we think about quitting the Christian's cause so did the early Disciples when Christ was crucified. However, the words that Christ spoke to them about His dying on the cross broke their hearts. Christ's death on the Cross seemed to shatter their lives. However, as Satan sought for Christ's suffering to alienate these Disciples from Jesus, this only solidified their unity and purpose. Armed with the Holy Spirit, their work became the foundation of the Church that thrives and fulfills its purpose throughout this great country that we live.

We too are human. Not every ministry will be one of notoriety as Peter's, John the Baptist's, Paul's, and others. Remember that God sees and understands (Heb. 4: 13), (Prov. 5: 21-23), (Exodus 3: 7). Turn someone's world upside down this week (Acts 17:6) by telling them about Jesus Christ. The early Disciples were given the opportunity to be a part of a "work" that would change the world! Christians today are given the opportunity to also be a part of the same "work" that will change people's lives with one credible witness at a time!

#56

STORY FOR THE HEART

UTILIZE TIME WHILE THERE IS TIME

I recently preached a message from the Book of Daniel regarding life in Ancient Babylon for God's captive people, Israel. When I reviewed this message, as I would hope each Christian would for each message that he or she hears preached or taught, I realized even more its significance to people everywhere.

The background for the message is established in Daniel, chapter four. King Nebuchadnezzar, who is historically noted as one of the world's greatest kings, had a dream that none of his soothsayers and astrologers could interpret. Daniel, a young Hebrew slave brought to Babylon during one of Nebuchadnezzar's kingdom expanding adventures, interpreted the king's dream through God's intervention. According to Daniel's interpretation, King Nebuchadnezzar had been given his kingdom by God, Himself, and not of the king's own efforts. Yet, because of the king's defiance toward God in ruling his kingdom, he would be temporarily relieved of his kingdom, lose his mind for a specific time and be driven out from others to eat grass with the cattle (Dan.4: 32-34). When his mind returned to him, he praised and extolled God Almighty and his kingdom was restored (Dan. 4: 35-37).

Certainly, knowing all that had happened to his father, Belshazzar, Nebuchadnezzar's son, is as much or even more defiant to God when he inherited his father's throne. Belshazzar is given a vision of a man's finger writing on his palace wall, and the message is not favorable. Once again, astrologers and soothsayers cannot interpret the vision. The queen, who remembered Nebuchadnezzar's experiences, encouraged Belshazzar to call for Daniel who had interpreted his father's dream and thus may possibly interpret Belshazzar's vision.

The relevance of this message to each Christian and each Christian church is threefold. First Belshazzar was in trouble with God. So are countless family members and friends of people who faithfully attend church today. Secondly, although Belshazzar admitted that he had heard of Daniel and his God (Dan. 5: 14), it was not until the queen established greater credibility that helped make the difference in Belshazzar's thinking. Certainly, one would be hard pressed to find people in our country who have not heard about God, heaven, and hell. Yet, as in Belshazzar's situation, maybe the right person has not witnessed to him to help make God more credible. Thirdly, for Belshazzar, the queen's message was too late. For those who have died without God, it is too late for them also.

Many people often think that it is darkest before dawn. This may not only be true physically, but also spiritually. Christians, who have lost loved ones, need to share their testimonies with those closest to their hearts. Although loved ones are surely aware of God's Son, Jesus Christ, who was sent to seek and save those who were lost (Luke 19:10) (John 3 16), maybe the right person has not yet witnessed to them to help make God's message more credible as was in the situation with the queen and King Belshazzar? Who is more credible to be listened to than a son, daughter, sister, brother, father, mother, or one's closest friend?

#57

STORY FOR THE HEART

THE LIABILITIES OF A WEAKENING WITNESS

In Mark 5: 1-20, Jesus and His Disciples had, the evening before, crossed over the Sea of Galilee to the land of the Gadarenes on the eastern side. Upon arriving on the shore of the Gadarenes, Jesus was immediately met by a man who lived among the tombs, there, having been possessed by an unclean spirit (vs. 2). The people who lived in this country had often tried to bind him with fetters and chains to no avail. Because of his condition, he cried aloud and cut himself with stones both day and night (vs.4-5).

Upon seeing Jesus from afar, the man ran to Jesus and worshipped Him. After Jesus commanded the demon to come out of the man, the demon called out to Jesus, "What have I to do with Thee, Jesus, Thou Son of the most high God? I adjure Thee by God, that Thou torment me not (vs. 7). The demon told Jesus that his name was Legion, for there were many of them.

After being removed from the man's body, the demons begged Jesus not to send them out of the country. Instead, they asked Jesus to cast them into a nearby herd of swine (vs. 10-11). Jesus agreed to do so for the demons, and they entered in the herd of swine that consisted of about 2000. When this occurred, the entire herd ran violently into the sea and drowned (vs. 12-13).

Those people who had been caring for the swine were shocked at the occurrence and ran into the city and told all what had happened. Those told came out to see for themselves. Upon arriving, the people saw the man that had been possessed with the devil, sitting, and clothed, and in his right mind, and THEY WERE AFRAID (vs. 14-15).

When the people from the city saw the man who was now sitting in his right mind, they questioned as to how this miracle had occurred. They also were told that the healing of the man was associated with the drowning of the swine. When they fully understood the circumstances of what happened, they together, prayed that Jesus would depart out of their coasts (vs. 16-17).

As Jesus cooperated with the people's request to leave, He entered again the ship that had brought Him from the other side. Upon doing so, the man who had been cured asked Jesus if he could go with Him. Jesus told the man to go home to thy friends and tell them how great things the Lord hath done for thee, and hath had compassion on thee (vs. 18-19).

The man, now healed, did as Jesus requested him to do. He went into the city of Decapolis and began to testify throughout the city how great things that Jesus had done for him. ALL men that heard his testimony were astonished and MARVELED (vs. 20).

What a marvelous miracle did Jesus perform on this man of the tombs. There was a great need existing in this country of the Gadarenes by the very existence of "many demons" presently living there, and their requests not to send them out of this country. How tragic that an entire country possessed by demons chose to remain demon controlled except for one man. How compassionately did Jesus react, by crossing the Sea of Galilee knowing that He would be able to help only one. The people living there had made several attempts at trying to help the possessed man by putting him in "chains and fetters". This act was undoubtedly to restrain him from fear that he might injure them and not necessarily wanted to provide some relief from his condition.

It is hard to imagine that the people of Decapolis had not heard of Jesus' ministry around the Sea of Galilee. If so, why did not at least one person of Decapolis, who sincerely wanted to help this possessed man, travel across the sea and diligently search the Master for help. The people's insincerity was finally accented when they realized that the possessed man was now healed at the "expense of the loss of a herd of swine". They, meaning all, asked Jesus to leave before He would undoubtedly do something further to cause more "financial loss".

In all their evaluation of the results of the miracle, their concern for the possessed man had undoubtedly been solely for the danger that he presented. The fear of his potential threat revealed that their concerns were primarily focused on their own lives, their own needs, and maintaining their own possessions.

PEOPLE LIKE YOU

People who live in fear do not have their trust in Jesus (2 Tim. 1: 7). To undertake such measures to "help" another person with his need is admirable and like Christ. However, if the underlying reason for helping is solely for one's personal benefit rather than to truly seek positive change, this is most unacceptable.

Regarding the people of Decapolis, their selfish intentions are realized by the comparison of the people's concerns for the man in relation to that of the swine. Sadly, to ask Jesus to leave their coasts revealed a total ignorance of God as the people were no doubt blinded by the power of Satan. It should be noted that the blinding of an entire city would not be achieved in just a short time. The condition of the people's hearts had without a doubt, progressively hardened as less and less of them resisted ungodly values presented by the blinding of their minds.

Where was the focus of the minds of the people of Decapolis? It is noted in the Scripture that Jesus crossed over the Sea of Galilee knowing that He would be able to help only one. Were there no other individuals needing a miracle? Surely the multitudes that followed Jesus and witnessed His working of miracles publicized these wonderful experiences everywhere they traveled. Could the same people of Decapolis who bound the possessed man "to help him" have either silenced others or driven them from their city; out of sight is often viewed as out of mind.

Any failure of any people to deny compassion to give assistance to a neighbor in need is denying the teaching of Christ. To exercise selfishness with God's gifts to us of time, talent, and treasure, we expose a "chink" in our armor that surely will be noticed by Satan.

Jesus said that "ye will have the poor with you always" (Matt. 26:11). This is stated to remind humanity that there will always be a friend or neighbor who needs assistance (1 Cor.10: 24). Love thy neighbor as thyself (Mark 12: 31).

God's people have opportunities to help others daily. If this assistance is genuine, then it is probably noted in the portals of Heaven as a sowing or watering of a seed for the advancement of a ministry for the Lord (1 Cor. 3: 6-9). Undoubtedly, the people of Decapolis had long ago abandoned their sowing and watering skills. This was evident when they **all**, blinded by the power of Satan, asked the Master to leave their city.

Many Americans are becoming obsessed with "grasping the good life, in living the American dream". Building a life without including Jesus Christ is like building a house upon sand. "When the rains descended and the floods came, the winds blew, and beat upon that house; and it fell: and great was the fall of it".

Jesus also added that, "Whosoever heareth these sayings of mine, (Bible truths) and doth them, I will liken him unto a wise man, which built his house upon a rock: and the rain descended, and the floods came, and the winds blew, and beat upon that house; and it fell not: for it was founded upon a rock " (Matthew 7: 15-29).

The Bible clearly states that we have only one life here on earth, and then judgment to determine where our "next life" shall be (Hebrews 9: 27). A reservation is needed to live eternally in a place that "eye hath not seen, nor ear heard, nor entered into the heart of man what God hath prepared for them who love Him (1 Cor. 2:9), (Rom. 10: 9-10), (Jn. 3: 16), (Luke 23: 43), (Matt. 25:41). Here, again is a reminder to get your reservation (Amos 4: 9-12), (Haggai 1: 2-11)!

#58

STORY FOR THE HEART

DO YOU KNOW ANY
GOOD NEWS TO SHARE?

The story about Noah and the Ark is well known to the young and not so young alike. It is retold in children's Sunday school classes repeatedly in churches throughout the world. It would be tragic, however, if the underlying spiritual values were overlooked, because the event was to be viewed only as a story for children.

The Bible states that Noah was 500 years old when his sons, Shem, Ham, and Japheth were born (Gen. 5:32). God points out to Noah that "it repented Him that he made man on the earth," because man's every thought was continually evil (Gen. 6: 5-6). Man's reluctance in God's eyes to repent and follow God's ways would cost mankind a high price (Gen. 6:13, Rom. 6:23).

God tells Noah to build an ark that would be needed to sustain not only his own family's lives, but the animals required to take as well.

(Gen. 6: 13-17). Only Noah, his wife, sons, and daughters-in-law would be spared.

When the Ark was constructed, Noah was to place on board clean and unclean animals (Lev. 11) to propagate the animal creation. Fully loaded, Noah and his family boarded the ark and waited for seven days for the rain to begin (Gen. 7:10).

The Bible states that the Windows of Heaven were opened, and the flood was on the earth for 150 days (Gen. 7:24, 8:2). God sent a wind to accomplish the drying of the land (Gen. 8:1).

Landing on Mt. Ararat, those aboard the ark departed, and Noah prepared an offering to God expressing his gratitude (Gen. 8: 20-21). Even though God had just executed fierce judgment on mankind with great climax, He still expressed His incomprehensible love for His creation "by remembering Noah and his seed (Gen. 9:12-13).

The values derived from this story for strengthening Christian character are unmistakable. First, Noah, ALONE, found grace in God's eyes. Often, we find ourselves seemingly alone and weak in God's service. Assuredly, none of us could ever realize the loneliness that Noah experienced. Thus, STANDING ALONE should NOT DETER US from Christian service. Secondly, our reluctance to repent and seek God's purpose for our lives will cost us greatly today as it did to mankind then. We are no match for Satan who seeks to devour any who totter with temptations unacceptable to God. God is ALWAYS waiting quietly and patiently for His children to CALL HIS NAME and SEEK HIS WILL (Luke 11:9). Thirdly, the vessel that Noah was instructed to build, was by man's standards not seaworthy by any means; it was too long (450 feet), too narrow (75 feet), and too tall and top heavy (45 feet) (Gen. 6:15).

Again, we are to understand that GOD'S WAYS are NOT OUR WAYS (Heb. 3:19). We are not asked to DEVISE PLANS for successful ministries, but to FOLLOW PLANS he has prescribed for us (Mark 1:17). Although there are many other lessons to learn from this story, certainly Christians today can realize that through faith, JUST ONE PENITENT, FORGIVEN, and RIGHTEOUSLY DIRECTED CHRISTIAN has the potential to accomplish the UNBELIEVABLE. One may be asked to attempt the seemingly IMPOSSIBLE, wait for the uncertainty of the IMPROBABLE, but always experience the assuredly INEVITABLE. Let us as Christians, never forget that God will keep HIS PROMISES. Through the PRESENCE and POWER of the HOLY SPIRIT, let us work to keep OURS!

#59

STORY FOR THE HEART

IT'S "SAFE" TO NOT ALWAYS SPEAK "OUT"

I was in church one day when Jake R. Multon was to deliver the Sunday morning sermon. The topic was "jumping to negative conclusions". As he discussed several incidents from his life's experiences, I could not help but remember some regrettable incidents in my own life when I had spoken inappropriately about someone in an unjustifiably negative way.

He ended his message by telling a story when he was working with the telephone company located here in Clayton County. He had been given a request from his superiors to go to a home in a remote area of the county to acquire written permission to locate a telephone pole on the person's property. Upon arriving at his intended destination in the company truck and dressed in his company uniform including his hard hat Jake exited his vehicle and with his request in hand, began walking toward the house. Sitting on the porch in a swing was a man that Jake assumed was the owner and person to see. As he approached the porch, a woman stepped out of the house to meet Jake.

Jake began to introduce himself and explain the reason for his arrival. Suddenly, the woman interrupted him and said, "I know who you are. You are Jake Multon, the pastor of Villander Baptist Church."

"Well, yes, I am," replied Jake. Once again, as he began to detail the reason of his arrival, the woman again interrupted him.

Speaking in a firm, authoritative tone, she exclaimed, "Do you see that man sitting over there in that swing? I want you to know that I have been living here with him for over two years, and I have not slept with him ONE TIME! Do you hear me?"

Having a most difficult time withholding a smile, Jake replied, "That is admirable of you, ma'am. However, I am just here to acquire permission to set a telephone pole on this property."

There are many times when people often say something that is regretful. Sometimes, what is said is not necessarily what is intended.

The Bible states that "whatsoever is in the heart cometh out of the mouth" (Luke 6: 45). There are two rules that I consider when choosing my words wisely before speaking. The first rule is often regrettably noticed; once words are spoken, they cannot be taken back. The second rule to follow is just as pointed; too often one's heart can speak faster than the brain can tell the mouth to stop what is to be said!

I am an avid sports fan of just about any sport. Because I have umpired many baseball and softball games, I have watched the reaction of umpires intently when having to make a close call of out or safe. Almost invariably when the call is made, there is a one to two second delay between the play and the call from the umpire. This is probably to allow for the mind to process the play and correctly decide either out or safe. If people, especially Christians, would do more processing before speaking, their testimony may be more likely considered "safe" for listening to and not necessarily "out" of tune with the God that they profess.

#60

STORY FOR THE HEART

PREPARING FOR BATTLE AGAINST THE ENEMY

On November 14, 1970, the Marshall University football team was returning from North Carolina after playing a football game against East Carolina. Just before entering the Huntington Tri-state Airport in Ceredo, West Virginia, upon approach, crashed into the hillside killing all 75 people aboard. This tragedy is the deadliest of any sports accidents ever recorded in the United States. The movie, "We Are Marshall", produced by McG. in 2008, is a factual reproduction of this tragedy.

Amazingly, the following year, 1971, the Marshall Sports Program reinstated its football program under first year coach Jack Lengyel. The record of the football team for the season 1971 was two wins and eight losses.

The above facts are probably the most important in giving an accurate summary of the return of the football program at Marshall University after the devastating plane crash. There is one noted occurrence that many people may not be aware of, that is most noteworthy.

The new first year coach of the 1971 football season had very little experience regarding offensive and defensive strategies. To receive some assistance in his coaching, Lengyel needed a "playbook" to follow. Possibly, in one of the boldest requests in sports history, Lengyel sent a message to head football coach, Don Nehlen, at West Virginia University, requesting the use of Nehlen's football "playbook" for Lengyel's 1971 football schedule.

To Lengyel's surprise, Nehlen agreed and sent a copy of his "playbook" to Lengyel. This one act of assistance from Nehlen, reflected his character and elevated his name as one of the most admirable coaches in West Virginia University history (The Herald Dispatch, Huntington, WV).

As I thought on the consequences of having someone else's "playbook" of strategies used upon its opponents, I thought of Christians and their struggles against Satan, a real adversary (1 Peter 5: 8-9). Would having Satan's "playbook" as to his strategies against Christians be most helpful in thwarting Satan's attacks and advances upon our lives?

Anyone can easily access Satan's playbook of strategies from reading the Bible. One story that is interesting illustrates strategies used by Satan on God's children. In this story Satan is foiled by a young teenager who saves his King and his armies?

The story of David and Goliath is found in the book of 1 Samuel 17. As the story unfolds, David is just a youth taking care of his father's sheep on the hills of Bethlehem in Judea. The armies of the

Philistines have entered the land belonging to Israel and readied themselves for battle. As chapter 17 unfolds, the army of Israel has had to gather itself opposite to the Philistines on an opposing mountain and prepare for a Philistine attack. It should be noted that the Philistines had already learned the art of metallurgy, separating iron ore from its impurities. Thus, they had at their disposal the making of swords, chariot wheels, armor, shields, and other items. God had kept this knowledge unknown to Israel promising them that He would be their shield and safety (Psalms 115: 9), (Psalms 89: 18), (2 Samuel 22: 3).

As the sun rises in Shochoh, its rays flash the brilliance of shiny metal emanating from the presence of the Philistines army on the mountaintop. The **intent was to intimidate the Israelites by striking fear in the hearts of those in the armies of Israel.** This was further shown by the presence of Goliath, **a nine feet tall giant** who approaches Israel's army daily blaspheming God's children. A second strategy of Satan included **transferring Israel's hope for deliverance from God's intervention to focusing their hope in King Saul** to deliver them.

God's children today, need to be reminded that Satan is a created angel and is not omnipotent, omniscient, and omnipresent as God the creator exists. At one time Satan led a revolt in heaven to overthrow God's rule (Isaiah 14:13). A war resulted and Satan and a third of the angels in heaven were cast out unto the earth (Rev. 12: 4). As a result of this expulsion, Satan reminds God daily of His failed creation (Rev. 10: 12) and walks upon the earth to destroy mankind (1 Pet. 5: 8).

God encourages mankind that no weaponry formed will harm His children (Isaiah 54: 17), and that with every attempt to destroy them, God will provide for them a way of escape (1 Cor. 10: 13). God's children are to resist Satan and he will flee (James 4: 7), and that, within each of God's children, is the Power to do the impossible (Luke 1: 37), (Phil. 4: 13). A faithful and obedient life in Jesus Christ promises abundant blessings here without measure (Mal. 3: 10) and immortality (John 3: 16), (John 10: 28) in a place that eye has not seen, nor ear heard, nor entered the heart of man what God has prepared for them who love Him (1 Cor. 2:9).

Again, in the story of David and Goliath as recorded in 1 Samuel chapter 17, Satan has encouraged the Philistine army to enter the land of Israel to destroy God's children. After **40 days of repeated threats by Goliath** to terrorize and **frighten** God's children to **self-destruct**, God sends David (1 Cor. 10: 13), to rescue His children. Today, as then, God seeks a deliverer to rise and lead His children in various places to do battle against Satan.

Let us today, knowing that Satan is still trying to destroy God's children, resist Satan's attacks as David did, "Who is this . . .who defies the armies (God's children) of the Living God (1 Sam. 17: 26)?

Satan feared the God of Israel, as was verified by the **40-day delay,** exit, and destruction of the Philistine army. David would become King of Israel for 40 years and would do battle with the Philistines the rest of his lifetime.

Christians today, filled with the Holy Spirit, create fear in Satan as did David. Each believer needs to be aware that **as David was**

called to lead God's children into battle, **so may we be called to do also**. The **number of soldiers that we are to lead is immaterial**.

Read God's Word! In the Scriptures, we know that we have the **promises** of God: **His strength** (Phil. 4: 13); **His presence** (Matt.8: 20); **His blessings** (Jeremiah 29: 11); **God hears our prayers** (John 14: 13-14); **God will fight for us** (Exodus 14: 14); **God will give us an Inner Peace** (John 14: 27); **God promises to Never Leave Us Alone** (Matt. 28: 20).

Let us do and say as David spoke unto the enemy (Satan), "Thou comest unto me. . . but **I comest unto thee in the name of the Lord** of hosts, the God of the armies of Israel; this day will the Lord deliver thee into mine hand, that all may know . . . that the battle is the Lord's (1 Sam. 17: 45-46).

In just the lifetime of one generation, I personally have witnessed a "changing of the guard" in America's belief, **"In God We Trust"**! Winston Churchill, quoted George Santayana in a speech in the British House of Common when he stated, "Those who fail to learn from history, are doomed to repeat it." The people of the United States of America may falsely believe that God will not exercise His Judgment on them as He has done on every generation of people in the past. Sadly, and tragically, they will believe wrongly with the results being fatal.

Life, as we are accustomed to living, is nearing extinction. All people, especially those who profess His name, need to prepare for His return to earth (1Thes. 4: 13-18) and get their house in order (2 Kings 20: 1). While living on this earth, Jesus promised His followers that He was going to go prepare a place for them to live with Him.

In the same verses, Jesus told them that He would return to receive them unto Himself (John 14: 1-6).

Let us today, as **Christians and guardians** of the **keys to the door of Eternal Life** (Matt. 16: 19), realize that Satan is even more so **today,** seeking how he might destroy **our families** (Rev. 13: 18) (1 Peter 5: 8).

Let us awake from our slumber (Rom. 13: 11**). Let us attire** ourselves with the **full armor of God that we may stand between our loved ones and the powers of evil** (Eph. 6: 10-18). **Let us pray** to the Father that we may be strong enough to **proclaim** to those dearests to **our hearts** that **they will be safe** (Isa. 41:10), (Matt. 25: 23), (Jn. 16-33), (Jn. 14: 3), (Rom. 8: 18).

Let us seek to be strong and have **good courage in Jesus Christ** (Deut. 31: 6), (Ps. 31: 24), (Josh. 1: 9), (Ps. 56: 3-4). **Then and only then,** can we **stand firmly against the forces of evil through Christ** and **proclaim that our children and grandchildren will be safe on OUR WATCH!**

The **next event** to be scheduled **on God's calendar for mankind** will be the sound of a Trumpet to announce that God's children are leaving town. Thereafter, a call will be issued for heaven and earth to appear before the Judge of all Earth. Results of those in attendance will be final and penalties will extend forever without end (Rev. 20: 10), (Matt.25: 46), (2 Thess. 1: 9), (Matt. 26: 41), (Gen. 18: 22-25). **Subpoenas will not be required!**

ABOUT THE AUTHOR

L. Michael Schoonover is a 71-year-old retired elementary school teacher, principal, and former pastor from a small town in rural West Virginia. He grew up on a farm, in a Christian family with two older sisters and one younger brother. His Christian father and mother provided the discipline, guidance, and necessary work ethics needed for surviving in an ever changing, unforgiving world.

It was L. Michael's father who anchored the home in God's values, extending the blessing at all meals. Before any of the family retired in the evening at bedtime, his father would pray aloud for the watch care of the heavenly Father upon the family while faithfully thanking God for the blessings and care for the past day.

Reminiscence of oversized gardens providing more than adequate free produce for those near and far is vividly remembered from times spent with his mother. Relatives, friends, and neighbors periodically congregated at the farm for not only produce, but Christian fellowship through the sharing of musical talents.

The joint efforts of several Christian women, led by his mother, would always prepare a smorgasbord of food for the unscheduled, "after church service get togethers" on the farm. Children played and laughed loudly. Gospel music echoed from his mother's pounding of the piano. Guitar pickers would join in as everyone, but the small children harmonized hymns from the heart. It was a "loud and rowdy time" for the Lord's children! (Dion Boucicault, 1820-1890).

It is for the memory of his mother and father that L. Michael dedicates this book. May all who read this book, enjoy it as much as L. Michael did, in penning the words under the auspices of God, Himself.

Made in the USA
Columbia, SC
03 August 2024